GIRL'S GUIDE TO PUBERTY

Helping Girls 8–12 Understand Body Changes, Emotions, and Self-Care

LESLEY ADAMS

TABLE OF CONTENTS

Introduction.. 10

Chapter 1: The First Signs—What's Happening to Me? 16

What Is Puberty? 19

First Signs: Breast Buds, Body Odor, and Growth Spurts 21

Breast Buds... 22

Body Odor.. 23

Growth Spurts: Stretching Upward 24

Continuing Mia's Story 25

Your Time to Reflect 27

My Puberty Journal.................................... 27

Chapter 2: All About Periods—What You Need to Know.. 30

What Is a Period?... 33

Myth vs. Fact: Period Truths........................ 34

Signs Your First Period Is Coming 36

White Discharge in Your Underwear 36

Breast Development 36

Body Hair... 37

Growth Spurt 37

Emotional Changes 37

What to Do When It Happens 38

Step 1: Find Period Products........................ 38

Step 2: Use a Pad 39

Step 3: Tell Someone You Trust.................... 39

Handling Period Emergencies 40

Tracking Your Period 40

Managing Cramps and Discomfort 41

When to Talk to a Doctor 41

Choosing the Right Period Products 42

All About Period Products 43

Pads 43

Tampons 44

Period Underwear 45

Continuing Lena's Story 46

Your Time to Reflect 49

My Period Journal 49

How I Feel About Getting My Period 49

My Period Emergency Plan 49

Questions I Want to Ask: 50

Lena's Journal Page...50

Remember.. 51

Chapter 3: Hygiene and Self-Care—Feeling Fresh and Confident 52

Why Hygiene Is More Important Now 56

Soap vs. Body Wash: What's the Difference? 57

All About Deodorant and Antiperspirant 58

Taking Care of Your Underarms 59

Foot and Shoe Odor Solutions.............................. 60

Clothing Choices That Help Reduce Odor................. 61

Smart Laundry Habits 62

No Rewearing Sweaty Clothes 62

Taking Care of Your Skin and Hair 62

Simple Skincare Routines 63

Hair Washing Guidelines...64

How Often to Wash Your Hair.....................................65

Choosing the Right Products..66

Continuing Mia's Story 67

Your Time to Reflect 70

My Hygiene Routine Checklist....................................70

My Personal Hygiene Kit...72

Journal Prompts..72

Mia's Checklist..72

Self-Care Beyond Basic Hygiene 73

Chapter 4: Emotions and Mood Swings—Why Do I Feel This Way? **75**

Why Do I Feel So Emotional?.......................................77

The Science Behind Your Emotions...........................77

How to Manage Mood Swings 79

Creating a Personal "Calm Down Toolkit".................79

Talking About Feelings Instead of Bottling Them Up..... 80

How to Identify and Name Different Emotions..............81

Conversation Starters for Talking to Friends About Emotions 83

How to Talk With Parents or Trusted Adults About Emotions 85

Continuing Jasmine's Story...86

Self-Reflection Section.. 88

My Emotional Toolkit 88

Example: Jasmine's Three Core Strategies.................89

Chapter 5: Changing Friendships—Finding Your Place **91**

Why Do Friendships Change During Puberty? 93

How to Handle Disagreements and Drama 95

Identifying Healthy vs. Unhealthy Friendship Behaviors
....95

Recognizing and Avoiding Gossip and Rumors............97

Conflict Resolution Steps 99

Being True to Yourself 100

Understanding Your Values and Preferences 101

Building Confidence to Express Your Genuine Opinions
....102

Dealing With Peer Pressure in Friendships 103

Making New Friends Who Share Your Interests...........104

Ways to Maintain Your Identity Within a Friend Group
....106

Continuing Sofia's Story 107

Self-Reflection Section...110

My Friendship Values Worksheet..............................110

Journal Prompts..112

Sofia's Reflection 112

Friendship Inventory 113

Balancing Friendships and Personal Needs 113

Chapter 6: Body Confidence and Self-Love 115

Accepting Your Changing Body.......................................117

How to Handle Comments About Your Body From Others
....119

Unexpected Comments From Classmates or Friends 120

Well-Meaning but Hurtful Comments From Family
Members..120

Comments From Adults in Authority (Like Coaches or
Teachers) 121

Comments on Social Media...121

When Body Concerns Need Extra Support.................122

Finding Body-Positive Role Models............................123

Building Confidence From the Inside Out 124

The Connection Between How We Treat Our Bodies and How We Feel About Them 125

How to Practice Genuine Self-Care and Self-Kindness 126

Continuing Emily's Story.......................................128

Self-Reflection Section...130

Three Things I Love About Myself............................130

Journal Prompts...131

My Personal Strengths 131

Emily's Reflection..132

Media Reality Check..133

Changing the Conversation in Your Head 133

Chapter 7: Standing Up for Yourself—Knowing Your Worth..135

What Is Body Autonomy?.....................................137

Setting Boundaries With Confidence 138

Practical Strategies for Identifying Personal Boundaries 139

Different Types of Boundaries...............................140

Physical Boundaries 140

Emotional Boundaries.......................................140

Social Boundaries 140

How Boundaries Might Change in Different Situations .141

Identifying Your Non-Negotiables vs. Flexible Boundaries..142

Saying No and Meaning It 143

The Difference Between Being Nice and Being a Pushover 143

How to Overcome People-Pleasing Tendencies 144

Dealing With Guilt After Setting Boundaries 145

Continuing Ava's Story 146

Your Time to Reflect 148

My Personal Boundaries Worksheet 148

When It's Hard to Say No 150

Practice Your Boundary Statements 151

Ava's Reflection 151

Confidence-Building Affirmations 152

Chapter 8: Navigating the Journey of Growing Up 154

What Does Growing Up Mean? 156

The Balance Between Freedom and Accountability 158

Common Fears and Misconceptions About Growing Up 159

Setting Goals for Yourself 161

Short-Term vs. Long-Term Goals 161

Identifying Your Interests and Strengths 162

Breaking Big Dreams Into Smaller Steps 163

Trying New Things to Discover Passions 163

Learning From Setbacks and Mistakes 164

Practical Tools for Goal Achievement 165

Vision Boards and Visual Reminders 165

Finding Mentors and Role Models 166

Embracing Who You Are 167

Building a Positive Self-Image During Times of Change 167

Appreciate Your Body for What It Can Do, Not Just How It Looks 169

Continuing Lily's Story 171

Your Time to Reflect 173

    Letter to My Future Self 173

    Journal Prompts.. 174

    My Future List 175

    Lily's Letter to Her Future Self (Example) 176

    My Growing Up Journey 177

    My Special Qualities 177

Conclusion **179**

References **181**

INTRODUCTION

The sun blazed in a cloudless sky, forcing Lola to shield her eyes as she sat on the warm concrete steps of her front porch. Sweat trickled down her neck, and the metal watch on her wrist felt hot against her skin. She twisted her ponytail around her finger and checked the time one last time. Rachel was late again.

Just when Lola was about to go inside for a glass of lemonade, she spotted Rachel turning the corner. She was walking slowly, not running and waving excitedly like she usually did.

"Hey," Rachel said quietly as she reached the steps. "Sorry I'm late."

Lola scooted over to make room. "It's okay. Are you all right? You look kind of sad."

Rachel shrugged and dropped her backpack. "I guess. My mom took me shopping yesterday for new clothes."

"That sounds fun!" Lola said. "I love getting new stuff."

"It wasn't fun," Rachel mumbled. "None of my old shirts fit anymore, and Mom made me try on a million different ones. Then she said..." Rachel's voice dropped to a whisper, "She said I needed to get a training bra soon."

Lola's eyes widened. "Oh. Wow."

"Yeah." Rachel pulled at the hem of her new purple T-shirt. "Do you have one?"

Lola shook her head. "No. But my sister Jade got her first one when she was our age."

"Does that mean we're growing up for real?" Rachel asked.

"I think so," Lola replied. "My mom says everyone changes at different times. She told Jade not to worry because she was almost thirteen when she started noticing changes."

Rachel sighed, looking a little relieved. "That makes me feel better. I thought I was weird for starting early. I'm only eleven."

"My sister says there's no 'right' time," Lola said. "Just your time."

They sat in silence for a minute, watching a butterfly land on a nearby flower.

"Have you noticed anything different about yourself?" Rachel finally asked. "Like, changes?"

Lola thought for a moment. "Not really. But I did get taller. My dad measured me on the kitchen doorframe last week, and I grew an inch since my birthday."

"I've been feeling weird lately," Rachel admitted. "Sometimes I get super angry at my little brother for no reason, and then I feel like crying five minutes later. My mom says it's normal, but it doesn't feel normal."

"That happens to Jade, too!" Lola exclaimed. "Last week, she yelled at me for borrowing her hairbrush, and then later, she came into my room and hugged me and said sorry like a hundred times."

"Did she say why she felt that way?"

"Yeah. She said sometimes her feelings get really big, like they're too much to keep inside, so they come bursting out. She said it's part of growing up."

Rachel nodded slowly. "My mom said something like that, too. She said my body is starting to make new chemicals called hormones that can make my feelings stronger."

"That sounds kind of scary," Lola said.

"It is! And there's more stuff too," Rachel continued. "I have these weird bumps under my nipples that hurt sometimes, especially if I run a lot in gym class."

"Oh, that sounds painful."

"It's not too bad, just weird and different." Rachel glanced at Lola. "Did Jade tell you about other changes?"

Lola nodded. "Yeah. She showed me this book she got. It's all about puberty. It had drawings and everything."

"My mom wants to have a 'special talk' with me this weekend," Rachel said, making air quotes with her fingers. "I bet it's about all this growing up stuff."

"Probably," Lola agreed. "My mom had that talk with Jade. Jade said it wasn't as embarrassing as she thought it would be."

"I hope not." Rachel picked at a loose thread on her new shirt. "I just wish things could stay the same sometimes, you know? Being a kid is easy."

"But being grown up has good parts," Lola pointed out. "Like, my mom lets Jade stay up later. And she can go to the mall with her friends without a parent."

"That's true," Rachel said, looking a little happier. "My cousin Tia is fourteen, and she gets to wear makeup now."

"See? Not all bad," Lola said with a smile. She stood up and brushed off her shorts. "Want to go inside? My mom made cookies this morning."

Rachel grinned and grabbed her backpack. "Race you to the kitchen!"

As they dashed inside, laughing, both girls momentarily forgot about training bras and hormones and all the changes coming their way.

You're not alone if you've ever had a conversation like Lola and Rachel. Growing up comes with lots of questions, and sometimes it can feel confusing or even a little scary. That's okay! Every single person goes through these changes—it's a normal part of life.

When you grow up, you go through many, many changes. Some you can see, like getting taller or developing breasts. Others happen inside your body, like new feelings and emotions that can sometimes feel extra strong—happy one minute, upset or angry the next.

This time in your life has a name: puberty. It's when your body slowly changes from a kid's body into a grown-up's body. These changes don't happen overnight—puberty usually takes several years. Think of it like a really long movie that plays very slowly, with new scenes happening bit by bit.

Every girl goes through puberty, but we don't all start at the same time. Some girls notice changes as early as 8 years old, while others might not see much happening until they're 12, 13, or even later. That's completely normal and nothing to worry about!

In this book, we're going to talk about all these changes—both the ones everyone can see and the ones only you can feel. We'll explain why they happen, what you might expect, and most importantly, how to take care of yourself during this time.

This book is pretty much a helpful guide that has all of the information that you might be curious or worried about if you're between 8 and 12 years old. We are going to talk about everything: from how your body changes on the outside, to how you start to feel different on the inside. We will also answer questions you might be too shy to ask out loud, and we'll give you tips on how to handle all the new things you'll experience.

Other things that we will cover are about the early parts of growing up, like when your breasts start to grow, when you get body hair, when you grow taller quickly, and when you get your first period. We will also talk about feelings, friends, and how to take care of yourself during this time.

Keep in mind that this book is not for older teenagers who want to know about dating, sex, or later body changes. If you're 13 or older, you might already know the things in this book. There are other books made just for teens that talk about what you might want to know.

We won't cover topics like sex, having babies, or birth control in this book. Instead, we focus on helping you understand and feel good about the normal changes that happen when you first start growing up. We want to give you just the right amount of information for your age; not too little, and not too much.

Remember in the end that growing up happens to everyone, and though it might seem complicated sometimes, you're never alone in what you're feeling. Let's learn about it together!

CHAPTER 1: THE FIRST SIGNS—
WHAT'S HAPPENING TO ME?

Mia brushed her teeth in front of her bedroom mirror before school. She paused mid-brush when something caught her eye. She leaned closer to the mirror and pulled her pajama top tightly against her chest.

"That's weird," she whispered through a mouthful of toothpaste.

Two small bumps stuck out under her nipples that definitely hadn't been there before. She poked one gently and winced. It felt a little sore. Worry fluttered in her stomach.

"Mia! You're going to be late!" Her mom's voice echoed up the stairs.

"Coming!" Mia spat out her toothpaste and rushed to get dressed.

She grabbed her favorite blue T-shirt with the glittery star from the closet and pulled it over her head. The shirt fit differently across her chest. It used to hang straight down, but now it curved slightly outward where the little bumps were. No one else would probably notice, but to Mia, it looked like a big change.

During math class, questions filled Mia's head instead of fractions: *What was happening to her body? Should she tell someone? Would the bumps keep growing?*

At lunch, her best friend Zoe talked about their upcoming dance recital.

"I can't wait to wear our costumes!" Zoe bounced in her seat. "They sparkle so much under the lights!"

Mia looked at Zoe while she talked. Her friend's chest was still flat under her T-shirt. A funny feeling came over Mia. She felt different now, like her body was changing while Zoe's stayed the same.

"Mia? Hello?" Zoe waved a hand in front of Mia's face. "Are you listening?"

"Sorry," Mia blinked. "I was thinking about something."

"What?" Zoe asked.

Mia opened her mouth, then shut it again. The noisy lunch table didn't feel like the right place to talk about her body.

"Just thinking about our math homework," she said. "Are you going to eat that cookie?"

That evening, Mia sat on her bed, hugging her knees. The questions in her head had gotten bigger throughout the day. She remembered what her teacher, Ms. Jackson, always said: "When you don't know something, ask someone who can help."

Mia stood up. Her mom would know what was happening.

"Mom?" Mia walked down the stairs. "Can I talk to you about something?"

Mom looked up from her laptop. "Of course, honey." She closed her computer. "What's up?"

"I noticed something different about my body," Mia said, pointing to her chest. "There are little bumps here, and they weren't there before."

Mom smiled. "Those are called breast buds. They're usually the first sign that your body is starting to grow up."

"Like puberty?" Mia asked.

"Exactly. Your body is starting to change and grow. It happens to all girls, but not all at the same time."

"Zoe doesn't have them yet," Mia said.

"Everyone starts at their own time," Mom explained. "I was about your age when I first noticed changes."

"So, it's normal?" Mia asked.

"Completely normal," Mom gave her a hug. "I'm glad you talked to me. Do you have questions?"

"A lot of them," Mia said.

"How about we start with a few tonight, and tomorrow I'll find a good book that explains everything? We can read it together."

"Thanks, Mom." Mia hugged her back, feeling much better. She wasn't weird after all—just growing up.

What Is Puberty?

Just like Mia, you might notice your body starting to change. These changes mean you're starting puberty! Puberty is the time when your body slowly changes from a child's body into an adult's body. It doesn't happen overnight, though. It's like a very slow movie that plays out over several years.

During puberty, your body makes special chemicals that we call hormones. Hormones are like tiny messengers that travel through your blood and tell different parts of your body that, "Hey! It's time to grow up!" The most important hormone for girls is estrogen, and it helps your body know how to change.

Puberty can start at different ages for different girls. Some girls notice their first changes as early as 8 years old, while others might not see changes until they're 11 or 12. Some girls might even start a little later, and that's completely normal too! Your body has its own special timeline that's just right for you.

Here are some of the main changes you can expect during puberty:

- You will grow taller, sometimes really quickly.

- Your breasts will start to grow, beginning with small bumps called breast buds.

- Hair will start to grow in new places, like under your arms and in your private area.

- Your body shape will change, with your hips getting wider.

- Your skin might get oilier, and you might get pimples.

- You'll start to sweat more and might notice body odor.

- At some point, you'll get your first period (we talk about this more in the next chapter).

- You might have new feelings and emotions that can sometimes feel very strong.

These changes don't all happen at once! They happen little by little over several years. Some changes might happen quickly, while others take their time. And not every girl goes through puberty in exactly the same way or in the same order.

The most important thing to know is that these changes are normal, natural, and happen to every single person. Even though it might feel a little weird or confusing sometimes, it's all actually pretty amazing. It shows your body is healthy and growing just the way it should!

First Signs: Breast Buds, Body Odor, and Growth Spurts

Mia sat alone on her bed that night, thinking about her talk with Mom. She pulled out the small notebook she kept hidden under her mattress and wrote:

Today I learned about breast buds. That's what these little bumps under my nipples are called. Mom says they're normal and the first sign that my body is growing up. She says everyone gets them at different times. Zoe doesn't have them yet, but that's okay.

Mia paused and tapped her pencil against her chin.

Mom also said there are other changes I might notice soon. She mentioned body odor (which sounds gross) and growing taller really fast (which sounds awesome). She said I might grow out of my favorite shoes before they even wear out!

I'm still not sure how I feel about all this. Part of me is happy to be growing up, but another part wishes things could stay the same for a little longer. Mom says that's normal, too.

Mia closed her notebook and slid it back underneath her mattress. Tomorrow, she and Mom would look at that puberty book together. She had a lot of questions, but knowing Mom would help her understand made her feel better.

Let's talk about these first signs of puberty that you might notice in your own body:

Breast Buds

Remember how Mia noticed the small, tender bumps under her nipples? Those are called breast buds, and they're usually the first sign that your breasts are beginning to develop.

- Breast development happens in stages, and it takes several years from start to finish. Every girl's timeline is different, but here's what you can expect:

- First, you'll notice small, sometimes tender bumps under your nipples. These bumps might feel a bit sore if you bump them or press on them. This is completely normal! These breast buds are just the beginning of your breast tissue growing.

- Next, your nipples and the dark skin around them (called the areola) might get a little bigger and maybe a shade or two darker. This is your body's way of preparing for the changes ahead.

- Then, over the next few years, the breast tissue will slowly grow outward. Your breasts will start to get rounder and fuller, but they won't grow to their full size right away. This happens very gradually!

- You might notice that your breasts grow at different speeds. One might look bigger than the other for a while. Don't worry about this! Almost all women have slightly different-sized breasts, and during development, this difference can be more noticeable.

Body Odor

Sometimes, you'll be sitting in class or playing with your friends, and out of the blue, you notice a smell. You'll sniff around and wonder where it's coming from, and then realize—oh no—it's coming from you!

This is totally normal! When puberty starts, your body starts making a new kind of sweat, especially under your arms and in other places where you have skin folds. This sweat is different from the kind you made when you were younger.

Here's what happens: Your body has two types of sweat glands. The ones you've had since you were a baby make clear, watery sweat that doesn't smell much. But during puberty, another type of sweat gland wakes up and starts working. These glands make a thicker type of sweat that has proteins and oils in it.

This sweat doesn't actually smell bad when it first comes out of your body. But tiny germs that live naturally on your skin mix with this sweat, and that's what creates the smell. It's kind of like how food doesn't smell until you cook it. The germs are "cooking" the sweat.

The good news is that body odor is super easy to manage! Here's how:

- Take a shower or bath every day, especially after you've been active or sweaty.

- Use soap to wash under your arms and anywhere else you notice smells.

- Dry yourself well after bathing (germs love moisture!).

- Put on clean clothes every day, especially clean underwear and socks.

- Use deodorant under your arms (ask a parent or other trusted adult to help you choose one).

Growth Spurts: Stretching Upward

Have you ever woken up and felt like your pajama pants suddenly shrank? Or maybe your shoes feel snug after just buying them a few months ago? That could be a growth spurt!

Your body grows faster than it has since you were a tiny baby. Many girls grow 2–3 inches in just one year during their big growth spurt! This usually happens at the beginning of puberty, often before your first period.

Growth spurts can happen in surprising ways. You might notice your feet growing first, then your legs get longer, and finally, your torso (the middle part of your body) catches up. This can make you feel a bit clumsy for a while, like your body parts aren't quite in sync. Don't worry—your body is just growing in stages, not all at once!

Here are some signs you might be having a growth spurt:

- Your pants suddenly seem too short.

- Your shoes feel tight or uncomfortable.

- You feel funny twinges in your legs, especially at night.

- You feel hungrier than usual.

- You might feel extra tired (growing takes a lot of energy!).

- Your joints might feel a little achy.

During a growth spurt, your body needs lots and lots of healthy food to support all that growing. Your body is building new bones, muscles, and other tissues, which requires lots of nutrients. That's why you might feel super hungry sometimes!

You might also notice those funny twinges in your legs, especially at night. They're usually little aches that come and go. They're not serious, but they can feel uncomfortable. Gentle stretching, warm baths, or a cozy heating pad can help if you get those funny twinges.

No matter when you grow or how tall you become, your height is mostly decided by your genes—the special instructions passed down from your parents. So if your parents or grandparents are tall, you might grow tall too! But if they're shorter, you might be shorter as well. All heights are perfectly normal!

Continuing Mia's Story

Later that evening, Mia and her mom sat on Mia's bed with mugs of hot chocolate. Earlier, Mom had promised that they would have a longer conversation about all the changes Mia was experiencing. The bedroom felt cozy and safe. Mia had closed the door so her little brother wouldn't barge in.

"I looked up some information after you talked to me this afternoon," Mom said, setting her mug on the nightstand. "I wanted to make sure I could answer all your questions."

"So, is that what happened to you, too, Mom?" Mia asked, pulling her knees up to her chest. "Did you get breast buds when you were my age?"

25

Mom nodded. "Yes, I was about your age when I first noticed my breast buds. I was so confused because none of my friends seemed to be changing yet."

"That's exactly how I feel!" Mia exclaimed. "Zoe doesn't have any changes at all, and I was worried something was wrong with me."

"Nothing's wrong with you," Mom assured her. "Actually, your sister Jade started developing early, too. It runs in our family."

"Really? Jade never told me that," Mia said, surprised.

"Well, it's not something everyone likes to talk about," Mom explained. "Jade was pretty private about it when she was your age. But I bet if you asked her now, she'd tell you about her experience."

Mom reached into her bag and pulled out a colorful book. "I got this for you today. It explains everything about puberty in a way that's easy to understand. We can look at it together, or you can read it on your own—whatever makes you comfortable."

Mia took the book and flipped through the pages. It had friendly pictures and stories about other girls going through the same things.

"There's a section about breast buds right here," Mom pointed out. "And look, it talks about all the other changes you might notice soon."

Instant relief washed all over Mia. Seeing everything explained so well made it seem less scary and strange.

"Can I keep this in my room?" she asked.

"Of course," Mom smiled. "And anytime you have questions or notice something new happening, you can always come talk to me. Or Jade. Or even Grandma—she helped me when I was your age."

Mia nodded, already feeling better. She wasn't weird or different. She was growing up, just like her mom and sister had before her.

"So... is it okay if I get a sports bra like Rachel has?" Mia asked. "For gym class?"

"I think that's a great idea," Mom said. "We can go shopping this weekend if you want."

Mia hugged the book to her chest. What had seemed so weird and scary this morning now felt like just another part of growing up. She wasn't alone after all.

Your Time to Reflect

My Puberty Journal

Just like Mia keeps a journal about her changing body, you can, too! This is your private space to write down your thoughts, feelings, and questions.

Questions to Think About
- *Have I noticed any changes in my body yet? What are they?*

- *How do these changes make me feel?*

- *Who are the grown-ups I trust to talk to about puberty?*

- *What questions do I still have about growing up?*

My Changes Chart
Draw or write about any changes you've noticed in yourself.

Things I've noticed:

_____

_____

_____

_____

How these changes make me feel:

_____

_____

_____

_____

Remember These True Things
- Your body is growing exactly as it should.

- Everyone develops at a pace that is perfect.

- It's okay to feel excited, confused, or both!

- You are never alone in this journey.

Mia's Journal Page

Dear Journal,

Today was a big day. I finally talked to Mom about the breast buds I found yesterday. I was really nervous at first, but Mom was so nice about it. She didn't laugh or make me feel weird.

Things I learned:

- *The bumps are called breast buds .*

- *They're supposed to be there—nothing is wrong!*

- *Our family tends to develop early.*

- *Zoe not having them yet is normal, too.*

How I feel:

I feel SO much better now! This morning, I was scared that something was wrong with me. Now I understand this is just part of growing up. Mom got me a book about puberty, and we're going shopping for sports bras this weekend (yippee!). I might even talk to Jade about it since Mom says she went through the same thing.

Questions I still have:

How long until my breasts grow more? Will I get taller soon, too? When will I get my period?

Note to self:

It's okay to be different. We're all growing at our own speed!

Chapter 2: All About Periods—What You Need to Know

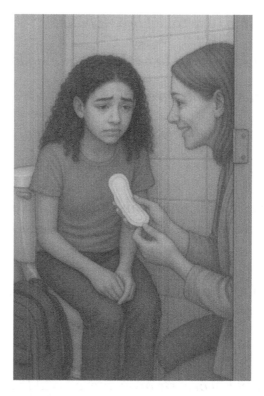

L ena shifted uncomfortably in her seat during math class. Her stomach felt weird, not painful, but achy and crampy. She was fine at breakfast, but now something didn't feel right.

"Lena, would you like to solve the next problem?" Mrs. Garcia asked.

"Um, sure," Lena said, trying to focus while she walked to the whiteboard. As she worked through the fraction problem, the crampy feeling got worse. She quickly finished the math problem and hurried back to her seat.

When lunchtime came, Lena really needed to use the bathroom. She stood up from the cafeteria table, and her friend Maya asked, "Are you okay? You look kind of pale."

"I'm fine," Lena replied. "Just need the bathroom. Will you save my seat?"

When she was in the bathroom stall, Lena gasped. There was a reddish-brown stain in her underwear! Her heart started racing. Was she bleeding? Was something wrong? Then suddenly, she remembered the puberty video they'd watched in health class last month. Is this her period?

"Oh no," she whispered to herself. "Not now. Not at school!"

She froze for a minute, unsure of what to do. She didn't have any pads with her. She wasn't prepared for this at all! And her light blue shorts might show a stain if she wasn't careful.

She folded some toilet paper into a pad shape and placed it in her underwear. It wasn't great, but maybe it would work until she got home. Then she tied her sweatshirt around her waist, making sure it covered the back of her shorts.

When she got to the cafeteria, Maya looked at her curiously. "Is everything okay?"

Lena almost told her friend what happened. Maya would probably understand. Her older sister had already gotten her period. But what if Maya told someone else? What if the boys found out? The thought made Lena's cheeks burn with embarrassment.

"I'm just not feeling great," Lena mumbled, picking at her lunch.

By science class, Lena was really worried. The toilet paper wasn't working very well, and she kept thinking everyone could somehow tell what was happening. When she went to the bathroom again, she noticed the stain had gotten bigger.

Finally, Lena made a decision. After science, she walked to the office instead of heading to her next class.

"Can I see the nurse?" she asked the secretary in a quiet voice.

A few minutes later, she sat across from Nurse Chen, taking a deep breath for courage.

"I think I got my period," Lena whispered, looking down at her shoes. "And I don't have any... you know... supplies."

Nurse Chen smiled a kind smile. "That happens to lots of girls, my dear. Getting your first period can be surprising, especially when it happens at school."

She opened a drawer and took out a small paper bag. "Here's a pad you can use right now. The bathroom is right through that door, and there are instructions on the package if you need them."

When Lena came back from the bathroom feeling much more comfortable, Nurse Chen gave her a few more pads to keep in her backpack.

"Would you like me to call your mom?" Nurse Chen asked.

Lena nodded, still feeling a little embarrassed but mostly relieved.

"While we wait for her to answer, let me tell you something," Nurse Chen said. "Every woman remembers her first period. Mine came during a piano recital! Getting your period is actually pretty amazing. It means your body is healthy and growing just like it should."

By the time Lena's mom arrived 20 minutes later, Lena was feeling much calmer. This is definitely not a disaster, just another step in growing up.

What Is a Period?

A period is when blood comes out of a girl's vagina (the opening between your legs). It usually happens once a month and lasts for about 3–7 days. The blood is usually reddish or brownish, which is different from the blood you see when you get a cut or scrape.

A period is part of something called the menstrual cycle, which is a pattern your body follows month after month. Here's how it works in simple terms:

- Every month, your uterus (the special organ inside your lower belly) gets ready for a possible baby by building up a soft, spongy lining that is made of blood and tissue. It's like your uterus is making a cozy nest, just in case.

- Most of the time, especially when you're young, no baby starts growing. When this happens, your body doesn't need that special lining anymore. So, the uterus sheds this lining, and it comes out through your vagina as your period.

- Then, the whole cycle starts over again! Your body begins preparing a fresh lining for the next month.

The time between one period and the next is usually about a month (around 28 days), but it can be longer or shorter. When you first start having periods, they might not come regularly at all! You might get one, then wait two months for the next one. This is completely normal. It takes about a year or two for them to become more regular.

Just remember, getting your period is a normal, healthy part of being a girl. Even though it might seem a little scary or messy at first, millions of girls and women deal with periods every day. And soon, you'll know exactly how to handle yours, too!

Myth vs. Fact: Period Truths

People will likely tell you all sorts of things about periods that just aren't true! Let's clear up some common mix-ups:

Myth: Everyone can tell when you have your period.

- **Fact:** Nope! No one can tell you're having your period unless you tell them. Pads and tampons don't show through your clothes, and periods don't make you look different.

Myth: You can't swim during your period.

- **Fact:** You absolutely can swim during your period! Water pressure actually helps hold the flow back while you're swimming, and you can use a tampon if you're comfortable with it.

Myth: Periods are always painful.

- **Fact:** Some girls have cramps or discomfort, and some hardly feel anything at all. If you do have cramps, there are lots of ways to feel better.

Myth: You lose a lot of blood during your period.

- **Fact:** Though it might look like a lot, most girls only lose about 2–3 tablespoons of blood during their entire period.

Myth: Having your period means you should avoid exercise.

- **Fact:** Exercise is actually great during your period! It can help reduce cramps and boost your mood. Just do whatever feels good to you.

Myth: If you get your period early, something is wrong.

- **Fact:** Girls can start their periods anytime between 8 and 16 years old, and it's all normal. There's no "right time" to get your first period.

Myth: Once you get your period, it comes exactly every 28 days.

- **Fact:** Very few girls have perfectly regular periods, especially in the first couple of years. Your period might come every 21 days, every 35 days, or be completely unpredictable at first!

Signs Your First Period Is Coming

Are you curious about when your first period will arrive? Well, your body usually gives you some clues! Most girls notice several other changes before their first period shows up. These signs can start anywhere from a few months to two years before your first period.

Here are the most common signs that your period might be coming soon:

White Discharge in Your Underwear

One of the earliest signs is finding a clear or whitish fluid in your underwear. This is called vaginal discharge, and it's completely normal and healthy! This discharge helps keep your vagina clean and protected. When you start noticing this regularly, it often means your first period could happen within the next 6–12 months.

Breast Development

Most girls develop breast buds (those small, sometimes tender bumps under your nipples) about 2–3 years before getting their first period. By the time your period arrives, your breasts have usually been developing for a while.

Body Hair

Hair growing in new places—like under your arms and in your pubic area (between your legs)—is another sign that your body is getting ready. This hair often appears about a year before your first period.

Growth Spurt

Many girls have their major growth spurt (when you grow several inches taller in a short time) right before their first period. If you've recently grown a lot taller, your period might not be far behind.

Emotional Changes

There are also other changes in your feelings that you will feel, including these:

- mood swings (feeling happy one minute and upset or irritable the next)

- feeling more emotional or sensitive than usual

- getting frustrated more easily

- feeling anxious or nervous for no clear reason

These signs are all different for everyone. Some girls don't notice any signs at all before their first period arrives. Your body works on its own schedule, and whatever way it happens for you is exactly right. The best way to prepare is to start carrying a small period kit in your backpack or locker once you notice some of these signs. We'll talk about what to include in that kit in the next section!

What to Do When It Happens

No need to panic! You're now joining billions of girls and women around the world who manage their periods every day. Your first period is actually pretty special. It's a sign that your body is healthy and growing just as it should. Even though it might feel a little overwhelming right now, you'll soon become a period pro who handles it with confidence.

Remember Lena from our story? She was pretty surprised and worried when her period started at school, but once she got help from Nurse Chen, she realized it wasn't such a big deal after all. Your experience might be different. Maybe you discovered your period at home, or maybe you'd already talked with someone about what to expect. However it happened for you, the important thing is knowing what to do next.

It's a lot like learning to ride a bike; you'll wobble and feel uncertain at first, but before you know it, it will be just another normal part of your life that you handle without even thinking much about it. Let's walk through exactly what you need to do now that your period has arrived.

Step 1: Find Period Products

You're going to need something to absorb the blood. If you're at home, ask your mom, older sister, or another trusted female relative for a pad. If you're at school like Lena was, you can

- ask the school nurse.

- talk to a female teacher you trust.

- ask a friend who might already have her period.

- check if the girl's bathroom has a pad dispenser (many do, so don't sweat it!).

Step 2: Use a Pad

Most girls start with pads, which stick to your underwear and catch the blood. Here's how to use one:

1. Unwrap the pad.

2. Remove the paper strip covering the sticky part.

3. Press the sticky side firmly to the inside of your underwear (in the middle).

4. Make sure the pad is flat and comfortable.

5. Change your pad every 3–4 hours, or more often if it feels wet.

Step 3: Tell Someone You Trust

You don't have to keep your period a secret! Tell your mom, dad, or another trusted adult. You might feel shy, but remember—they want to help you. You can simply say:

- "Mom, I just got my period today."

- "Dad, I need some supplies for my period."

- "Can you help me? I think I started my period."

Handling Period Emergencies

Accidents happen, and you might get in a situation where you get some blood on your clothes. When that happens, you can

- tie a sweatshirt or jacket around your waist.

- rinse the stain with cold water as soon as possible.

- ask an adult to help you treat the stain.

If you don't have any period products

- make a temporary pad from folded toilet paper.

- ask a female teacher, a nurse, or a friend for help.

Females will always understand and want to help you!

Tracking Your Period

After your first period, it's helpful to keep track of when it happens. This can help you predict when your next period will come. You can

- mark the days on a calendar with a special symbol.

- use a small notebook as a period diary.

- ask your parent about period tracking apps designed for young girls.

In the beginning, your periods might be very irregular—you might skip months or have two periods close together. This is totally normal! It usually takes 1–2 years for periods to become more regular.

Managing Cramps and Discomfort

If you have cramps or feel uncomfortable, here's what you can do:

- Use a heating pad or warm water bottle on your lower belly.

- Take a warm bath or shower.

- Try gentle stretching or walking.

- Rest when you need to.

- Ask a parent about taking pain medicine if the cramps are really bothersome.

- Drink plenty of water.

- Avoid super sugary or salty foods, which can make bloating worse.

When to Talk to a Doctor

Most period issues are completely normal, but talk to a parent about seeing a doctor if you experience any of the following:

- Your period lasts more than 7 days.

- You need to change your pad more than every 1–2 hours.

- Your cramps are so bad that you can't go to school or do normal activities.

- You feel very dizzy or extremely tired during your period.

- You go more than 3 months between periods after they've become regular.

- You have serious concerns or questions.

Choosing the Right Period Products

There are so many period products out there, it's like walking into an ice cream shop with 100 flavors when you just want a simple scoop of vanilla! All the colorful boxes and packages can make your head spin, but you know what? You don't need to know about all of them right now.

Pads are always the perfect starting point because they're easy to use and super helpful when you're new to this whole period business. Think of pads like training wheels on a bike. They give you confidence while you're learning!

As you get more comfortable with having periods, you might get curious about other options. Let's check out what's available and help you figure out what might work best for you.

All About Period Products

Pads

Pads are soft, special stickers that go in your underwear to catch period blood. They're the easiest product to use when you're first starting your period.

What pads look like: Pads look like rectangles of fluffy material with a sticky side that attaches to your underwear. The top side (the part that touches your body) is soft and gentle.

Different kinds of pads:

- **Thin pads:** These are about as thick as two pieces of paper stacked together. They're great for light days or when you're just starting your period.

- **Regular pads:** These are a little thicker than thin pads, like a thin cushion. Good for most days.

- **Thick pads:** These are cushier and can hold more blood for heavier days.

- **Overnight pads:** These are extra long to protect your underwear while you sleep and move around in bed.

- **Pads with wings:** These have little flaps (like tiny wings) that wrap under your underwear to help keep the pad from sliding around.

How to use a pad:

1. Wash your hands first.

2. Take the pad out of its wrapper.

3. There's a paper strip covering the sticky part; peel that off.

4. Stick the pad in the middle of your underwear (the sticky side goes against your underwear, not your body!)

5. If your pad has wings, fold them under your underwear to help keep everything in place.

6. Pull your underwear up and you're all set!

7. Change your pad every few hours, or when it starts to feel wet.

8. To throw away a used pad, roll it up, wrap it in toilet paper or the wrapper from your new pad, and put it in the trash can (never flush pads down the toilet!)

Tampons

Tampons are small cotton plugs that go inside your body to catch the blood before it comes out. Many girls don't start using tampons until they're a bit older and more comfortable with their bodies.

- **What tampons look like:** A tampon is a small tube of cotton that's about the size of your pinky finger. Most tampons come with an applicator, which is a plastic or cardboard tube that helps you put the tampon in the right place.

- **When you might want to try tampons:** Most girls start with pads and try tampons later when they want to do things like swimming during their period. There's no "right age" to start using tampons. It's about when you feel ready. Some girls start at 12 or 13, others wait until they're older.

- **How tampons work:** Tampons go inside your vagina (the opening between your legs where period blood comes out). The tampon sits inside your body and soaks up the blood before it can come out. A string hangs outside your body so you can pull the tampon out when it's time to change it.

Practice makes perfect with tampons, and that's okay! When you feel ready to try them, ask your mom or another trusted adult to help explain exactly how to use them.

Period Underwear

Period underwear looks just like regular underwear but has special layers inside that soak up blood so it doesn't leak through.

What period underwear looks like: From the outside, it looks exactly like regular underwear! But inside, it has hidden layers that can absorb blood and keep you dry.

How to use period underwear:

1. Put them on just like regular underwear.

2. Wear them all day (they can usually hold about as much as 2–3 tampons)

3. When you take them off, rinse them with cold water.

4. Put them in the washing machine.

5. Let them dry.

Continuing Lena's Story

The school day finally ended, and Lena was sitting in the passenger seat of her mom's car, with the paper bag from the nurse's office clutched in her lap.

"So," Mom said, glancing over at Lena, "Nurse Chen called and told me what happened. How are you feeling?"

Lena traced the edge of the paper bag with her finger. "Kinda weird. And embarrassed. I wasn't ready for it to happen at school."

"I bet," Mom nodded. "I got my first period during a family vacation. Talk about bad timing!"

"Really?" Lena looked up. "What did you do?"

"I told your grandma, and she helped me. Just like you told Nurse Chen, and she helped you." Mom reached over and squeezed Lena's hand. "I'm proud of you for handling it so well."

"I didn't handle it well at all," Lena groaned. "I stuffed toilet paper in my underwear and nearly had a meltdown in science class."

Mom laughed. "That's actually pretty resourceful! And you figured out who to ask for help, which must've taken a whole lot of courage."

Lena hadn't thought about it that way before. Maybe she had been braver than she realized.

When they got home, Mom took Lena to the bathroom cabinet and showed her where the pads were kept. "These are yours now," she said, pulling out a colorful package. "And I thought we could make you a little period kit to keep in your backpack so you're prepared next time."

They found a small zippered pouch that used to hold Lena's colored pencils. Mom helped her pack it with two pads, a clean pair of underwear, and a small package of wipes.

"What about at night?" Lena asked. "Nurse Chen mentioned something about overnight pads?"

"Good question," Mom said. "Let me show you the difference."

For the next half hour, Mom explained everything about periods that Lena had been too embarrassed to ask before. They talked about cramps and how to feel better if she got them. Mom showed her how to track her period on a calendar so she could start to predict when the next one might come.

"You know," Mom said as they finished their talk, "getting your period is actually pretty amazing when you think about it; it's a sign that your body is healthy and growing exactly as it should."

Lena wasn't sure she'd call it "amazing" just yet, but she did feel different than she had this morning—less scared and more... grown up, somehow.

That evening, as she got herself ready for bed, she looked at her reflection in the bathroom mirror. She was the same as yesterday; the only thing that had changed was that she had handled her first period. It had been scary and messy and uncomfortable, but she had gotten through it.

"I did it," she whispered to her reflection, standing a little taller.

The next day at school, Lena spotted Maya in the hallway.

"Feeling better?" Maya asked.

Lena took a deep breath. "Yeah. Actually, I got my first period yesterday."

"Really?" Maya's eyes widened. "Wow!"

"It was pretty scary at first," Lena admitted. "But the nurse helped me, and then my mom and I talked about everything."

"My sister got hers last year," Maya said. "She has this cool app on her phone that tells her when it's coming."

They walked to class together, and Lena realized that this thing that had seemed so embarrassing yesterday was just a normal part of growing up—something that would happen to Maya too, and all their friends, sooner or later. And now that she knew what to do, Lena felt ready. She even had her period kit zipped safely in her backpack, just in case.

She wasn't a little kid anymore, and for the first time, that felt like something to be proud of.

Your Time to Reflect

My Period Journal

This is a private place to write down your thoughts and feelings about periods.

How I Feel About Getting My Period

_____

_____

_____

_____

My Period Emergency Plan

Three trusted adults I can talk to about period questions:

1. _____

2. _____

3. _____

Places I might keep period supplies:

☐ backpack

☐ locker

☐ gym bag

☐ a friend's house

☐ Other:

_____

What I'll say if I need help while at school:

_____

_____

_____

_____

Questions I Want to Ask:

_____

_____

_____

_____

Lena's Journal Page

Dear Journal,

I got my first period yesterday at school! It was pretty scary at first. I wasn't prepared AT ALL and had to use toilet paper until I could talk to Nurse Chen. I was so embarrassed, but she was really nice about it and didn't make me feel weird.

Mom picked me up and we talked about EVERYTHING. She helped me make a period kit that I'm keeping in my backpack now. I feel so much better knowing I'm prepared for next time!

I even told Maya about it today. I was nervous to tell her, but she was cool about it. Her sister already has her period, too.

How I feel now:

Proud that I handled it, even though I was scared. A little nervous about getting cramps (Mom says they might not be bad since she never had bad ones). Excited that my body is growing up healthy!

—Lena

Remember

- Your period is a sign that your body is healthy and growing just as it should.

- Everyone's period experience is different—and that's perfectly normal!

- Getting your period doesn't change who you are.

- The more you know about your body, the more confident you'll feel.

- You're never alone—every woman you know has gone through this, too!

What will your period story be? However it happens, you'll handle it, just like Lena did!

Chapter 3: Hygiene and Self-Care—Feeling Fresh and Confident

"Hustle, hustle! Let's go, team!" Coach Martinez clapped her hands as the fifth-grade girls raced up and down the basketball court.

Mia dribbled the ball, dodging around Zoe and making a perfect pass to her teammate Leila. The ball swished through the net, and Mia jumped up for a high-five. She loved gym days when they played basketball. It was her favorite sport.

By the end of class, Mia's face glowed red from running, and her dark ponytail had mostly escaped its hair tie. Her gym shirt stuck to her back with sweat. It had been an awesome game—her team had won by six points!

"Good hustle out there, girls," Coach Martinez said as they lined up to head back to the locker room. "Remember to hydrate!"

In the crowded locker room, Mia chatted excitedly with Leila about their winning plays. She noticed Leila step back slightly as they talked. Weird, Mia thought, but didn't think much of it.

As they walked to their next class, Mia realized Zoe and Emma were walking a few steps behind her, even though they usually walked together. She slowed down to wait for them.

"Hey, wait up!" she called.

Zoe caught up but kept an unusual distance between them. Then, she leaned in close to Mia's ear and whispered, "Um, Mia? There's kind of a... smell. I think it might be coming from you?"

Mia froze. "What?"

"It's probably just your gym clothes," Zoe said quickly. "No big deal! But I thought you'd want to know."

Heat rushed to Mia's face, but not from running this time. She felt her stomach drop with embarrassment. Did she really smell bad? Had everyone noticed?

"I've gotta go to the bathroom," Mia mumbled, ducking away from her friends and rushing down the hall.

Inside a bathroom stall, Mia cautiously lifted the collar of her gym shirt and sniffed. She immediately pulled back, wrinkling her nose. Zoe was right. There was definitely a smell, kind of like onions or the way her dad's socks smelled after he went running. And it was coming from her!

How had she never noticed this before? Had she always smelled this way after gym class? Mia's mind raced with horrifying thoughts of everyone laughing behind her back for weeks.

When the bell rang, Mia quickly pulled her gym shirt away from her body and stuffed it deep into her backpack. She zipped it closed tightly, hoping to trap the smell inside.

For the rest of the day, Mia kept to herself. She sat at the edge of the lunch table instead of between her friends. In science class, she raised her arms extra carefully during an experiment, terrified that she still smelled. When the final bell rang, she rushed to catch her bus, avoiding her usual after-school chat with friends.

As the bus pulled away from school, Mia stared out the window, one burning question on her mind: What was happening to her body, and what was she going to do about it?

When she got home, Mia went straight to her room and closed the door. She carefully opened her backpack, holding it at arm's length as she removed the gym shirt. It still smelled bad, even worse now after being trapped in her backpack all afternoon.

She shoved the shirt deep into her hamper and flopped onto her bed, burying her face in her pillow. It wasn't fair! She'd always been a clean kid—she took showers, brushed her teeth, washed her hands. Why was her body suddenly betraying her like this?

"Mia? Are you home?" Her older sister Jade knocked on the door.

"Go away," Mia mumbled into her pillow.

Jade opened the door anyway and leaned against the doorframe. "What's up with you? Bad day?"

Mia sat up and looked at her sixteen-year-old sister. Jade always smelled nice, even after soccer practice. Maybe she would know what to do.

"Jade," Mia asked hesitantly, "did you ever... start to smell bad? Like, when you were my age?"

Jade's eyes widened with understanding, and she came into the room, closing the door behind her. "Ah. The body odor talk. Yeah, I remember those days."

As they headed to class, Mia felt a weight lift from her shoulders. Everyone went through these changes—even Zoe! And now that she knew what to do, she could handle it. Growing up might come with some embarrassing moments, but at least she didn't have to figure it all out alone.

After gym class that day, Mia used her deodorant and changed into her fresh shirt. When she joined her friends for lunch, no one stepped away or whispered. In fact, Leila even complimented her new strawberry-scented shampoo.

That evening, Mia made a checklist for her bulletin board: "Shower every day. Use deodorant. Change gym clothes. Wash gym clothes after wearing." It wasn't so hard after all. Just new habits to learn, like when she'd first started brushing her teeth by herself or doing her own hair.

"How was school today?" Mom asked as Mia helped set the table for dinner.

"Actually, it was pretty good," Mia replied, and she meant it. What had seemed like a huge, embarrassing disaster yesterday now felt like just another step on her journey to growing up—a journey she was starting to feel ready for.

Why Hygiene Is More Important Now

What you should know is that your body works differently as you grow up. The natural shifts that happen mean that you need to pay more attention to staying clean and fresh than you did when you were younger.

Your body now makes new hormones that cause your sweat glands to become more active. You actually have two different kinds of sweat glands:

First, there are eccrine sweat glands, which you've had since you were a baby. These are all over your body and make clear, watery sweat that doesn't smell much on its own.

But as you grow, your apocrine sweat glands wake up. These special glands are mostly in your armpits and private areas. They make a thicker type of sweat that contains proteins and oils. When this sweat mixes with the natural bacteria on your skin, it can create body odor.

Your skin also starts making more oil. This oil, called sebum, helps keep your skin and hair from getting too dry. But too much oil can make your hair look greasy faster and can lead to pimples on your face, back, or chest.

All these changes happen for good reasons! Your body is developing exactly as it should. The oils help protect your skin as you grow, and even body odor had a purpose long ago in human history (it helped people find mates. Weird but true!).

Soap vs. Body Wash: What's the Difference?

You have choices that you can think about when it comes to getting clean. It's pretty fun picking out what you like because you get to experience different products. It's like taking your senses on a marvelous adventure! Let's look at what works best:

- **Bar soap** is what many people think of first. It's solid, easy to use, and comes in many different scents. Some soaps are made especially for sensitive skin, while others have special ingredients to fight bacteria that cause odor.

- **Body wash** is liquid soap that is made up of moisturizers to keep your skin from getting dry. Many kids and teens prefer body wash because it's easy to use with a washcloth or shower pouf, and it comes in fun scents. Either soap or body wash works well for getting clean! The most important thing is to use something to wash your whole body, paying special attention to underarms, feet, and other areas that tend to get sweaty.

- **Antibacterial soaps** contain ingredients that kill more bacteria than regular soap. While this sounds helpful for fighting odor, most doctors say regular soap works just fine for everyday use. In fact, washing properly with any soap is more important than which type you choose!

All About Deodorant and Antiperspirant

Deodorant and antiperspirant are probably the most important products for managing body odor, but what's the difference between them?

- **Deodorant** works by killing the bacteria that make sweat smell bad. It doesn't stop you from sweating, but it does stop the smell. Most deodorants have a nice scent, so that means you'll smell fresh for a long time.

- **Antiperspirant** reduces how much you sweat by temporarily blocking your sweat glands. Less sweat means less odor! Many products are both a deodorant *and* an antiperspirant, so they fight odor in two ways.

- **When should you start using deodorant?** There's no specific age when everyone needs to start. The right time is when *you* start noticing body odor, especially after exercise or on hot days. For some kids, this happens at 8 or 9 years old, while others might not need it until 12 or 13.

- **How to use it:** Apply deodorant or antiperspirant to clean, dry underarms, usually in the morning after your shower or bath. Some people also apply it before bed for extra protection.

- **Finding the right product:** You might need to try a few different brands to find one that works best for your body. If one doesn't seem to be working well, don't be afraid to try another!

Taking Care of Your Underarms

Your underarms need special attention because they tend to get the most sweaty and smelly. Here's how to keep them fresh:

- **Washing:** Make sure to wash your underarms thoroughly with soap or body wash every day. Use warm water and don't rush. Give them a good cleaning!

- **Drying:** After washing, dry your underarms completely. Bacteria love moisture, so a dry underarm is less likely to develop odor.

- **Deodorant application:** Apply your deodorant or antiperspirant to completely dry underarms. Follow the directions on the package for how much to use.

- **About underarm hair:** During puberty, hair will start to grow in your underarms. This is completely normal! The hair can trap sweat and odor, so good cleaning becomes even more important.

- **Shaving (this is a personal choice):** Some people choose to remove underarm hair, while others don't.

This is entirely your choice! If you're interested in shaving, talk to a parent or other trusted adult first. They can help you learn to do it safely to avoid cuts or skin irritation. There's no "right age" to start shaving. It's about what makes you comfortable.

Foot and Shoe Odor Solutions

While most people think about underarm odor first, the truth is that feet can be the smelliest part of your body! Your feet have more sweat glands than almost anywhere else, and when all that sweat gets trapped inside socks and shoes, it creates the perfect environment for odor-causing bacteria to multiply. Even kids with great hygiene can develop stinky feet, especially if they're active or wear the same shoes every day. The good news is that foot odor is easy to manage with a few simple tricks and habits.

- **Daily washing:** Be sure to wash your feet every day with soap and water. Don't forget between your toes!

- **Dry thoroughly:** Moisture leads to smelly feet, so dry your feet completely after washing, especially between your toes.

- **Fresh socks daily:** Wear clean socks every day, and change them after sports or activities that make your feet sweat.

- **Sock materials:** Cotton socks or ones labeled "moisture-wicking" help keep feet drier than nylon socks.

- **Air out shoes:** Don't wear the same shoes every day. Let them dry out completely between wearings.

- **Shoe deodorizers:** You can use special sprays or powders made for shoes, or place baking soda in your shoes overnight to absorb odors.

- **Foot powder:** A little sprinkle of foot powder in your socks or shoes can help keep feet dry all day.

Clothing Choices That Help Reduce Odor

Did you know that what you wear can make a huge difference in how much you sweat and smell? Yup, that's because different fabrics act differently on your body; some help keep you cool and dry, while others can trap heat and moisture against your skin. Understanding these differences can help you make smart choices about what to wear, especially on active days or when the weather is hot. Making a few simple changes to your clothing choices can help you feel fresher and more confident all day long.

- **Natural fabrics:** Cotton, wool, and bamboo let your skin breathe and allow sweat to evaporate. These are great choices for everyday wear.

- **Synthetic fabrics:** Materials like polyester and nylon can trap heat and sweat against your skin, which can lead to more odor. Many sports clothes are made from special synthetic fabrics designed to wick moisture away. These are good for exercise but should be washed right after.

- **Loose vs. tight:** Looser fitting clothes allow air to circulate around your body, which helps sweat evaporate. Very tight clothes can trap sweat and increase odor.

- **Colors:** Dark colors show sweat stains less than light colors do. If you're worried about visible sweat marks, darker colors might make you feel more confident.

Smart Laundry Habits

Keeping clean isn't just about washing your body. Your clothes need regular cleaning, too! Many kids don't realize that clothes can hold onto sweat, oils, and bacteria even when they look clean. Developing good laundry habits now will help you manage body odor and keep your clothes looking and smelling fresh. Plus, knowing how to take care of your own clothes is an important skill that shows you're growing up and taking responsibility for yourself.

No Rewearing Sweaty Clothes

Even if your gym class was short, don't wear those clothes again without washing them first. Once clothes have soaked up sweat, they're a perfect place for odor-causing bacteria to grow.

Taking Care of Your Skin and Hair

If you talk to most teenagers and adults about growing up, they'll tell you that skin and hair changes were some of the first things they noticed. During these growing years, your skin might become oilier, and you might notice pimples for the first time. Your hair might get greasy faster than it used to. These changes are completely normal and happen to everyone! With the right care routine, you can keep your skin healthy and your hair looking its best throughout all these changes.

Simple Skincare Routines

You don't need a million products to take care of your skin! A simple routine with just a few steps works best for most girls your age. What's most important is being consistent. Washing your face every day will do more good than using fancy products once in a while.

Basic Routine for All Skin Types

1. Wash your face twice a day (morning and before bed) with a gentle cleanser.

2. Pat dry with a clean towel. Don't rub hard!

3. Apply moisturizer to keep skin from getting dry.

Use sunscreen during the day (many moisturizers include sunscreen).

If Your Skin Gets Oily

- Use a cleanser made for "oily skin" or "combination skin."

- Try an oil-free moisturizer.

- Use oil-blotting papers during the day if your skin gets shiny.

- Wash your face after sweaty activities.

If Your Skin Gets Dry

- Use a creamier cleanser labeled "for dry skin."

- Apply moisturizer while your skin is still slightly damp.

- Don't wash your face with hot water (warm is better).

- Consider using a thicker moisturizer at night.

If You Get Pimples

- Never pop or squeeze pimples (this can cause scars).

- Look for cleansers with salicylic acid.

- Keep hair products away from your face.

- Change pillowcases regularly.

- Wash your hands before touching your face.

Remember that everyone's skin is different, and it might take some time to figure out what works best for you. If you have serious skin concerns, talk to a parent about seeing a dermatologist (skin doctor).

Hair Washing Guidelines

Just like skin, your hair might start to change during your growing years. Many girls notice their hair gets oilier faster than it used to. How often you should wash your hair depends on your hair type and how active you are.

How Often to Wash Your Hair

- **For straight or fine hair:** This type of hair tends to show oil quickly because the oil from your scalp can easily travel down straight strands. Most girls with straight or fine hair need to wash every 1–2 days. If your hair is super fine, you might notice it looking flat or greasy by the end of the day.

- **For wavy or medium-textured hair:** Wavy hair typically doesn't show oil as quickly as straight hair. You can usually go 2–3 days between washes. On non-wash days, you might want to use dry shampoo (a powder spray that absorbs oil) at your roots if they start to look greasy.

- **For curly or coily hair:** Curly and coily hair often needs less frequent washing, sometimes only once a week. This is because the natural oils from your scalp take longer to travel down curly strands. Washing curly hair too often can make it dry and frizzy. Many girls with curly hair use conditioner more often than shampoo.

- **For active girls:** If you play sports or exercise regularly, you might need to wash your hair more often to remove sweat. Always wash your hair after swimming in pools because chlorine can damage your hair if left in too long.

Choosing the Right Products

Shampoo Types

- Regular shampoo works for most girls with normal hair.

- If your hair gets very oily, look for a "balancing" or "clarifying" shampoo.

- For dry or curly hair, choose a "moisturizing" or "hydrating" shampoo.

- If your hair is damaged from swimming or heat styling, try a "repairing" shampoo.

Conditioner Tips

Conditioner is important for all hair types! It helps make your hair soft and easier to comb. Apply conditioner after shampooing, focusing on the ends of your hair (not your scalp). Leave it on for a few minutes before rinsing out.

Hair Washing Steps

1. Wet your hair completely before adding shampoo.

2. Use about a quarter-sized amount of shampoo (more for longer hair).

3. Massage it into your scalp with your fingertips, not your nails.

4. Rinse thoroughly until the water runs clear.

5. Apply conditioner from mid-length to ends (avoid your scalp).

6. Comb through with your fingers or a wide-tooth comb while the conditioner is in.

7. Rinse well with cool water (cool water helps hair look shinier).

Remember that everyone's hair is different! Pay attention to how your hair feels and looks to figure out the best routine for you.

Continuing Mia's Story

That evening, after hiding in her room all afternoon, Mia finally worked up the courage to talk more with her sister. She knocked softly on Jade's bedroom door.

"Come in," Jade called.

Mia opened the door and hovered in the doorway. "Can we talk more about that... body odor thing?"

Jade patted a spot on her bed. "Of course. Come sit."

Mia sat cross-legged on Jade's bed, picking at a loose thread on the comforter. "So this body odor thing... it just happened all of a sudden. One day I was fine, and then today..." she trailed off, still embarrassed.

Jade nodded sympathetically. "That's exactly how it happened to me, too. I remember being so confused. I thought I was washing the same as always, but suddenly I smelled different."

"What did you do?" Mia asked.

"Well, Mom helped me, just like I'm helping you now," Jade said. "It's like a sisterhood initiation or something—everyone goes through it."

Mia smiled, feeling a little better. "So, what do I need besides deodorant?"

"How about we make a list, and then we can go to the store tomorrow after school?" Jade suggested. "You can pick out things you like."

The next day, Mia and Mom headed to the drugstore with their list. Mia had been nervous about the trip, worried someone from school might see her buying deodorant, but the store was mostly empty.

"There are so many choices," Mia said, staring at the wall of products. Some were in pink packages labeled "for girls," while others looked more grown-up.

"The pretty packaging costs extra," Mom explained. "What matters is finding something that works for you and that you'll actually use."

Mia picked up a deodorant that claimed to last 24 hours and smelled like fresh laundry. "I like this one."

"Good choice," Mom said. "Now let's look at some body wash."

They moved to another aisle where they found body washes in every scent imaginable. Mia chose one that smelled like watermelon.

"You'll want to shower every day now," Mom said. "Especially after basketball practice."

Mia nodded, trying not to feel overwhelmed by all these new changes.

"Oh, and let's get you a separate hamper for your dirty gym clothes," Mom added. "They need to be washed after each wear now."

By the time they checked out, they had a small collection of products: deodorant, body wash, a shower pouf, and a spray bottle of fabric refresher for her gym shoes.

That night, Mia established her new routine. She took a shower, washing carefully with her new body wash. After drying off, she applied deodorant just like Jade had shown her. She laid out fresh clothes for the next day, including her gym clothes.

"How's it going in there?" Mom called through the bathroom door.

"Good!" Mia replied, feeling proud of herself. "I think I've got it."

The next morning, Mia got up 15 minutes earlier than usual to give herself time for her new routine. By the time she arrived at school, she felt clean, fresh, and confident.

"Nice perfume," Zoe said as they walked to class.

"It's not perfume, it's just my body wash," Mia replied. "Watermelon."

"Cool," Zoe said. "My mom got me this strawberry one I really like."

As they chatted about scents they liked, Mia realized something important: these body changes weren't just happening to her. All her friends were going through the same thing or would be soon. It wasn't weird or embarrassing; it was just part of growing up.

After gym class, Mia used her deodorant and changed her shirt like she'd planned. No one stepped away from her or whispered about any smell. In fact, Emma even asked if she could borrow Mia's deodorant because she'd forgotten hers.

"Sure," Mia said, happy to help. Just yesterday, she'd been the one feeling embarrassed and unprepared. Today, she was sharing what she'd learned with a friend.

That night, Mia felt a small surge of pride as she checked off the items on her new hygiene checklist. Learning to take care of her changing body was just another step toward growing up—and she was handling it just fine.

Your Time to Reflect

My Hygiene Routine Checklist

Use this checklist to create your own personal hygiene routine! Check off the items that are important for your body, and add any special items you need.

Morning Routine
☐ Wash face with gentle cleanser.

☐ Brush teeth.

☐ Use deodorant/antiperspirant.

☐ Put on clean clothes.

☐ Brush/comb hair.

☐ Other:

_____

☐ Other:

_____

After-School/Activity Routine
☐ Change clothes if sweaty.

☐ Rinse face if needed.

☐ Reapply deodorant if needed.

☐ Other:

_____

Evening Routine
☐ Take a shower or bath.

☐ Wash hair (how many times per week? _____).

☐ Wash face.

☐ Brush teeth.

☐ Put on clean pajamas.

☐ Other:

_____

☐ Other:

_____

My Personal Hygiene Kit

List items you want to keep in your backpack, gym bag, or locker:

_____

_____

_____

_____

Journal Prompts

- *How do I feel when I'm clean and fresh?*

- *What scents make me feel happy and confident?*

- *What new hygiene habits are most important for me?*

- *What parts of my hygiene routine do I enjoy the most?*

Mia's Checklist

Morning Routine
☐ Wash face with gentle cleanser.

☐ Brush teeth.

☐ Use deodorant (fresh linen scent).

☐ Put on clean clothes.

☐ Brush hair.

- ☐ Pack a clean gym shirt in backpack.

After Basketball Routine
- ☐ Change into a clean shirt after gym.

- ☐ Reapply deodorant.

- ☐ Put sweaty clothes in a plastic bag.

- ☐ Spray fabric refresher in shoes if needed.

Evening Routine
- ☐ Take a shower with watermelon body wash.

- ☐ Wash hair (three times per week).

- ☐ Wash face.

- ☐ Brush teeth.

- ☐ Put on clean pajamas.

- ☐ Prepare clean gym clothes for tomorrow.

Self-Care Beyond Basic Hygiene

Taking care of yourself means more than just being clean! Try these ideas:

- Drink plenty of water to keep your skin healthy.

- Get enough sleep (9–11 hours for your age group).

- Take 10 minutes of quiet time when you feel stressed.

- Write down three things you like about yourself.

- Stretch your body after sitting for a long time.

- Listen to music that makes you happy.

- Talk kindly to yourself if you make a mistake.

Remember, good hygiene is a form of self-respect. When you take care of your body, you're showing yourself that you matter!

Chapter 4: Emotions and Mood Swings—Why Do I Feel This Way?

"So, I was thinking we could do our science project on how plants grow in different types of light," Jasmine said, spreading her notebook open on Zoe's bedroom floor.

Zoe wrinkled her nose. "Plants? Everyone always does plants. What about something with magnets instead?"

"But plants would be easier," Jasmine explained. "I already found this cool experiment with different colored light bulbs."

"Magnets are way cooler, though," Zoe insisted.

It was a small disagreement—the kind they'd had many times before without any drama. But today, something strange happened.

Jasmine felt a sudden tightness in her chest. Her throat got scratchy, and before she knew it, tears spilled down her cheeks.

"I just... really wanted to do the plants," she said, her voice catching.

Zoe stared in surprise. "Whoa, are you crying? Why? It's just a science project!"

Jasmine wiped her face, embarrassed. This made no sense. She wasn't a crier, especially not over something so small.

"I don't know what's wrong with me," she mumbled. "I'm not even sad."

"I'm going to use the bathroom," she said, quickly standing up.

In the bathroom mirror, Jasmine examined her blotchy face. Yesterday she'd snapped at her brother for no reason, and now these tears over a science project? It was like her emotions had a mind of their own.

"My sister went through this last year," Zoe explained when Jasmine returned. "She said her feelings got super-sized overnight. Mom said it was hormones."

"Hormones?" Jasmine repeated. She'd heard that word in health class but hadn't thought it applied to her yet.

"They make your emotions go crazy sometimes when you're growing up," Zoe said. "My sister cried when we got the wrong pizza toppings once."

Jasmine felt relieved. Maybe she wasn't losing her mind. Maybe this was just another part of growing up, like getting taller or needing deodorant.

Why Do I Feel So Emotional?

Emotions help us relate to the world around us. They are how we learn, connect with others, and understand ourselves. Everyone has emotions; they are what make us so wonderfully human, but the more you grow up, the stronger and more unpredictable they'll feel, like what happened to Jasmine in our story.

The Science Behind Your Emotions

Inside your brain, there's a part called the amygdala that processes emotions. During puberty, this part becomes more active. Meanwhile, the part of your brain that helps you think logically and control reactions (the prefrontal cortex) is still developing. This creates a temporary imbalance—strong emotions with less ability to manage them! Some of the emotional experiences that you'll likely feel along the way include:

- **Feeling everything:** One day you're watching a sad movie and you just start sobbing out of the blue, then next you're laughing like you've just heard the world's most ridiculous joke. It's like someone turned up the volume on your emotions!

- **Quick shifts between your emotions:** One minute you might feel on top of the world, and the next minute you feel down in the dumps—all without any major reason for the change. This happens because your hormone levels fluctuate throughout the day, affecting how you feel from moment to moment.

- **Crying easily:** Like Jasmine in our story, you might find yourself crying over things that wouldn't normally upset you. You might cry when you're not even sad; sometimes, when you're angry or frustrated instead! This doesn't mean you're weak or babyish. It's just your body's way of releasing emotional tension.

- **Easily irritated:** Small annoyances you used to brush off might suddenly feel incredibly frustrating. Your brother's chewing noise might drive you crazy, or a friend's harmless joke might make you feel angry. Your "irritation threshold" is lower during this time, making it easier to get upset.

Let yourself feel what you are feeling without shame. Your body and brain are going through big changes, and your emotions are just responding to those changes. In the next section, we'll talk about ways to manage these new, intense feelings.

How to Manage Mood Swings

"When I feel upset, I close my eyes, count to three, and ask myself this little question: 'Will this matter tomorrow?'" says Sophia, age 12. "It helps me figure out if I'm overreacting."

This is just one of many strategies that can help you handle the big emotions that come with growing up. Let's look at some practical ways to manage your mood swings and feel more in control of your feelings.

Creating a Personal "Calm Down Toolkit"

A "calm down toolkit" is just a collection of things that help you feel better when you're upset. You can make one easily with stuff you probably already have at home.

What you'll need:

- a box, bag, or special place in your room

- items that help you feel calm

Things to put in your toolkit:

- something to squeeze (like a stress ball or even a rolled-up sock)

- paper and colored pencils for drawing your feelings

- a favorite stuffed animal

- a family photo

- a list of three things that make you happy

- bubble wrap to pop

- a jump rope (moving your body helps with big feelings!)

- a card with "Breathe in for 4, hold for 4, out for 4" written on it

How to use your toolkit:

1. When you feel yourself getting upset, go to your toolkit.

2. Pick one thing that feels right for that moment.

3. Take a few minutes to use it.

4. Notice how you feel afterward.

Lucy, age 10, says: "When my brother makes me mad, I go to my room and jump rope for two minutes. Mom says it's because exercise helps get the angry energy out of my body. It works!"

You don't need fancy things to make a good toolkit; just items that help YOU feel better when emotions get big!

Talking About Feelings Instead of Bottling Them Up

Have you ever forgotten a sandwich in your lunchbox for a while? When you finally find it days later, it's probably pretty gross—maybe even moldy or smelly! Feelings can work the same way. When you try to hide them or ignore them, they don't just disappear. Instead, they can "go bad" inside you and cause bigger problems later.

Talking about your feelings is one of the most powerful tools you have for managing your emotions. When you share how you feel with someone you trust, those big, overwhelming feelings often start to feel smaller and more manageable. It's like opening a shaken-up soda bottle slowly instead of all at once. You release the pressure bit by bit, which is much safer than letting it build up until it explodes.

Finding the right person to talk to makes a big difference. This might be a parent, an older sibling, a trusted teacher, or a good friend. Different people in your life might be better for different types of feelings. Maybe your mom is great at helping you when you're sad, but your friend understands better when you're frustrated with school. The important thing is finding what works for you.

How to Identify and Name Different Emotions

A popsicle on a warm summer's day is one of the best things that could ever happen to you. Being able to put a word or a phrase to what you are feeling works just the same! When you can name your emotion, it immediately becomes less confusing and easier to handle.

Many of us use the same few words over and over to describe how we feel: happy, sad, mad, or fine. But emotions are much more colorful and complex than that! Learning more emotion words gives you more power to understand yourself. Think of it like this: If you only knew the words "red," "blue," and "yellow," you'd miss out on describing the beautiful purple sunset or the mint green of a leaf. The same goes for feelings. There's a big difference between feeling "annoyed" and "furious," even though both are types of anger.

Here are some feelings you might experience but not have names for yet:

Instead of just "happy," you might feel:

- excited: full of energy about something coming up

- proud: pleased with something you accomplished

- content: peaceful and satisfied

- relieved: glad something stressful is over

- hopeful: positive about what might happen

Instead of just "sad," you might feel:

- disappointed: let down because something didn't work out

- lonely: wishing you had company

- homesick: missing your familiar surroundings

- hurt: pained by something someone said or did

- melancholy: a quiet kind of sadness, like on rainy days

Instead of just "mad," you might feel:

- frustrated: blocked from reaching a goal

- irritated: bothered by small annoyances

- jealous: wishing you had what someone else has

- embarrassed: uncomfortable because of attention on you

- anxious: worried and nervous about what might happen

When you can name exactly what you're feeling, it's easier to know what to do about it. If you're "bored," you'll know that you might need to try a new activity. If you're "overwhelmed," it shows that you need to take a break. If you're "nervous," you need reassurance. Being specific helps both you and others understand what you really need.

Try this: The next time someone asks, "How are you feeling?" challenge yourself to use a more specific word than "fine" or "good." See if being more exact helps the other person understand you better!

Conversation Starters for Talking to Friends About Emotions

You likely want to approach a friend, but you're not sure how to bring up feelings without it being awkward. It can feel weird to suddenly start talking about emotions, especially if you and your friends don't usually have deep conversations. But sometimes sharing how you feel (or asking how they feel) can make your friendships even stronger.

Here are some easy ways to start conversations about feelings with friends:

- "I've been feeling kind of [nervous/excited/confused] about [situation]. Have you ever felt that way?"

- "Remember when [something that happened]? How did you feel about that?"

- "I noticed you seemed quieter than usual today. Is everything okay?"

- "Do you ever feel like your emotions are on a roller coaster sometimes?"

- "What's been the best and worst part of your day so far?"

- "If your mood was a weather forecast today, what would it be? Mine would be partly cloudy with a chance of sunshine later."

- "I read in this book that lots of kids our age have mood swings. Do you ever feel like that?"

The trick is to share a little bit about your own feelings first, which makes it safer for your friend to open up too. And remember, good friends don't judge each other's emotions or share private conversations with others.

Friends might not want to talk right away, and that's okay. Let them know you're there when they're ready, and then respect their space. True friendship means supporting each other through all kinds of emotions—the happy ones and the tricky ones, too!

How to Talk With Parents or Trusted Adults About Emotions

Talking to grown-ups about your feelings might seem hard sometimes. Maybe you worry they'll think your problems are silly, or you don't want to bother them when they're busy. But most adults in your life really do want to help; they just might not always know when you need them.

Here are some ways to start conversations with parents or other trusted adults:

- "Mom/Dad, do you have a few minutes to talk about something that's been bothering me?"

- "I've been feeling really [sad/angry/confused] lately, and I'm not sure why. Could we talk about it?"

- "Something happened at school that made me feel bad. Can I tell you about it?"

- "Did you ever feel like your emotions were really strong when you were my age?"

- "I read that it's normal to have mood swings when you're growing up. Is that true?"

- "I'd like to talk about something, but I'm not sure how to explain it."

If talking face-to-face feels too hard, try these alternatives:

- Write a note or letter to give to your parent.

- Send a text message if they're okay with that.

85

- Talk while doing an activity together (like walking the dog or riding in the car).

- Draw a picture that shows how you feel.

Pick a good time to talk when the adult isn't rushing or distracted. And remember that grown-ups might need a moment to think about what you're saying. They're still learning how to handle emotions, too!

If the first adult you talk to doesn't understand, try someone else. Sometimes, a teacher, school counselor, aunt, uncle, or friend's parent might be able to help, too. The important thing is to keep trying until you find someone who listens and helps you feel better.

Continuing Jasmine's Story

That evening, Jasmine sat at dinner pushing her peas around her plate, thinking about those unexpected tears at Zoe's house.

"You're quiet tonight," Mom said. "Everything okay?"

After dinner, while helping with dishes, Jasmine blurted out, "I cried today over nothing! We were just picking a science project, and suddenly I was crying like a baby. It was so embarrassing!"

"Ah," Mom nodded. "That sounds familiar."

"It does?" Jasmine stopped, surprised.

Mom led her to the couch. "When I was your age, I burst into tears because my friend borrowed my hairbrush without asking. My emotions felt too big for my body."

"That's exactly how I feel!" Jasmine exclaimed. "Like my feelings are taking over."

"It's part of growing up," Mom explained. "Your body is making new hormones that affect your emotions. It's completely normal, even though it doesn't feel normal."

Mom suggested some strategies: recognize early warning signs, take deep breaths, and they even created a code word—"butterflies"—for when Jasmine needed a moment to compose herself. Mom also suggested keeping a feelings journal.

Over the next week, Jasmine practiced these techniques. When someone cut in front of her in the lunch line, she noticed her face getting hot and took three deep breaths. When her brother broke her favorite pencil, she used their code word.

By the weekend, Jasmine had filled several pages in her journal and was starting to see patterns in her emotions.

"They actually help," Jasmine told Mom about the techniques. "I still feel things strongly sometimes, but I don't feel so out of control."

"I'm proud of you," Mom said. "It takes courage to face big feelings."

Jasmine smiled. "I think I'm learning more about myself. Like, when I write in my journal, I'm figuring out what really matters to me."

Maybe these big emotions weren't just something to manage—maybe they were also helping her grow into the person she was meant to become.

Self-Reflection Section

My Emotional Toolkit

This section is yours to build your strategies for emotional well-being throughout the seasons. You must reflect honestly and carefully on what works specifically for you, not what you think should work or what works for others.

Journal Prompts

- *When do I feel most emotionally balanced?* What elements, settings, or practices were present in those moments?

- *What patterns do I notice in my emotional responses across different seasons?* (For example: *Does winter bring particular challenges? Does summer energize or overwhelm me?*)

- *Which natural elements (earth, water, fire, air) do I instinctively turn to when seeking comfort or clarity?*

- *What practices from this book have resonated most strongly with my personal needs and preferences?*

My Calming Activities

Create your personalized list of practices that reliably help restore your emotional balance. Consider organizing these into categories:

- activities that take five minutes or less

- practices for different elements/settings (indoors/outdoors)

- strategies for specific emotional states (anxiety, sadness, overwhelm)

Example: Jasmine's Three Core Strategies

- **Taking five deep breaths before responding:** *When I feel reactive or defensive, this simple pause creates space between stimulus and response. I focus especially on making my exhales longer than my inhales, which helps activate my parasympathetic nervous system.*

- **Writing in my journal when feelings get intense:** *I keep my journal accessible at all times— bedside table, desk drawer, even a small one in my bag. Getting thoughts onto paper helps me see patterns I miss when emotions swirl internally.*

- **Going for a bike ride to clear my head:** *Movement is my medicine. Something about the combination of physical movement, changing scenery, and feeling wind against my skin helps reset my perspective when I'm stuck in circular thinking.*

If crying is what you need to do to help soothe the aching in your heart, then cry. If sitting quietly beneath trees helps you feel better, then sit. If putting your hands in garden soil makes you feel calm when everything seems too much, then dig. Nature doesn't have rules about how we should feel better; it offers different kinds of help for different kinds of hearts.

Try what feels right to you. Change things to make them your own. Create new ideas that come from your own adventures outside. Remember that the natural world has always been here for you, waiting patiently, ready to help whenever you need a place to feel safe, happy, or just more like yourself again.

CHAPTER 5:

CHANGING FRIENDSHIPS—

FINDING YOUR PLACE

Sofia poked at her lunch, watching the cafeteria chaos swirl around her. Normally, lunch period was her favorite part of the day—when she, Lily, and Madison would squeeze together at their usual table, sharing snacks and stories. But today, there was an empty seat between Lily on her left and Madison on her right.

"So, are we doing the park or the mall on Saturday?" Lily asked, breaking the uncomfortable silence as she unwrapped her sandwich.

Madison rolled her eyes. "I thought we decided on the mall already. Zoe and Aniya want to go to that new store that opened."

Sofia felt her stomach tighten. This was new territory—until a few months ago, the three of them had done everything together, just them. No outside friends, no separate plans, no divided loyalties.

"I didn't agree to invite Zoe and Aniya," Lily said, her voice taking on an edge Sofia recognized as trouble. "I thought it was just going to be us, like always."

"Well, that's kind of boring, don't you think?" Madison countered. "We always do the same things with the same people."

Sofia took a sip of water, wishing it could wash away the knot forming in her throat. When had things gotten so complicated? Last year, these lunch conversations had been filled with inside jokes and shared plans. Now every suggestion seemed loaded with invisible tripwires.

"What do you think, Sofia?" both girls asked in almost perfect unison, then glared at each other.

"I, um..." Sofia's voice caught. The truth was she didn't know what she thought anymore. Part of her understood Madison's desire to expand their circle, while another part shared Lily's comfort in their familiar trio.

The bell rang before she could form a response, bringing temporary relief. But as Sofia gathered her mostly untouched lunch, her phone buzzed twice in succession.

The first text was from Madison: *Lily's being so childish. You get why I want to include other people, right? You're on my side?*

Before she could respond, Lily's message appeared: *Madison's trying to ditch us for the popular girls. You're with me on this, right?*

Sofia stared at both messages, her thumbs hovering uncertainly over the screen. When had friendship become a battlefield with sides to choose? When had "us" fractured into competing camps, with her caught in the middle?

That night, Sofia lay awake long past her usual bedtime, staring at the glow-in-the-dark stars on her ceiling. She'd always thought friendship was the easy part of growing up. Now it felt like a test she hadn't studied for. What if she made the wrong choice? What if there wasn't a right answer at all? What if growing up meant growing apart from the people who knew the old you best?

The stars didn't give up any answers as Sofia turned over, pulling her blanket tighter around her shoulders. Why hadn't anyone warned her that friendships could get so complicated?

Why Do Friendships Change During Puberty?

We change when we get older, and that change often means that we are no longer the people we thought we were. The friends we played with every day in third grade might suddenly have different interests by sixth grade. One day you're building forts together, and the next day they're talking about things you don't really care about.

This happens to almost everyone during middle school, and it can feel really confusing!

When your body starts changing, your brain changes, too. You start liking different music, wanting to try new activities, or caring about different things than you did before.

Your friends are changing through all of this, too! But the tricky part is that they might be changing in different ways than you are. Your best friend might suddenly be interested in video games all the time while you're discovering that you love drawing comics. Or maybe they want to hang out with a new group of people while you're happy with your usual friends.

It's kind of like everyone is trying on different versions of themselves to see what fits best. This doesn't mean there's anything wrong with you or your friends. It's just part of figuring out who you really are.

Some friendships will grow stronger through these changes. Others might need some space. And you'll probably make some new friends who connect with the person you're becoming. All of these possibilities are completely normal, even when they feel uncomfortable.

How to Handle Disagreements and Drama

Disagreements are uncomfortable to deal with because when you speak up for yourself or share your true feelings, you might worry about hurting someone's feelings or making them mad at you. It's tempting to just agree with whatever your friends want or to pretend everything is fine when it's not. But learning to handle disagreements in a healthy way is an important skill that will help you build stronger friendships.

Identifying Healthy vs. Unhealthy Friendship Behaviors

We're first going to help each other understand what separates healthy and unhealthy friendship behaviors. Sometimes, it's hard to tell the difference when you're in the middle of a friendship, especially if things have slowly started to change. But there are some clear signs that can help you figure out if a friendship is helping you grow or holding you back.

Healthy Friendship Behaviors

- **Support and encouragement:** A good friend roots for you and inspires you to chase your dreams and to do everything to the best of your abilities. For example, if you want to try out for the school soccer team, a healthy friend will cheer you on and practice with you instead of saying you're not good enough.

- **Respect for boundaries:** Healthy friends understand when you need space. They won't make fun of you or call you names for being honest about what you need. If you have a big homework project and want to study alone, a supportive friend won't pressure you to play video games instead.

- **Honesty and communication:** In a healthy friendship, you can share your feelings without worry. If something they said hurt your feelings, a good friend will listen to you and talk it out rather than get upset.

- **Having fun together:** Healthy friends enjoy doing things together. If you both love playing games, you might spend weekends playing your favorite ones or having fun competitions.

Unhealthy Friendship Behaviors

- **Manipulation or control:** An unhealthy friend might try to tell you what to do. For instance, if they insist you skip school to hang out even though you don't want to, that's a red flag.

- **Constant criticism:** If your friend always makes fun of you or puts you down, it's not a good friendship. For example, if they tease you about your favorite sports team or make jokes about your interests, it can hurt your feelings.

- **Lack of support:** If your friend doesn't celebrate your wins or gets upset when you succeed, it's not healthy. For example, if you score a goal in a game and they just shrug it off, that shows they're not supportive.

- **One-sided efforts:** In an unhealthy friendship, you might feel like you're the only one trying. If you're always the one asking to hang out or make plans, and they never do the same, it's time to think about the friendship.

By noticing these signs, you can better understand your friendships and decide which ones help you feel happy and supported!

Recognizing and Avoiding Gossip and Rumors

Sometimes, we think we're making conversation, but what we're really doing is spreading gossip. Gossip happens when we talk about other people who aren't there, especially sharing information that might be private or unkind.

Here's what gossip might sound like:

- "Did you hear that Emma got kicked out of dance class?"

- "I heard Jayden's parents are getting divorced."

- "Don't tell anyone, but Mia told me she has a crush on Tyler."

Even if these things are true, sharing them can hurt feelings and damage friendships. It's important to recognize when a conversation has turned into gossip so you can choose not to participate.

Signs you might be gossiping:

- You're talking about someone who isn't present.

- You lower your voice or look around to make sure certain people don't hear.

- You use phrases like "Don't tell anyone, but..." or "Did you hear about...?"

- The information would embarrass the person if they heard you sharing it

- You feel a little uncomfortable or guilty about the conversation

Rumors are similar to gossip, but they're stories that might not even be true. Rumors can spread super fast, especially at school, and they can really hurt someone's feelings or reputation.

Maya learned this the hard way when she overheard someone saying her friend Olivia had cheated on a math test. Maya mentioned it to someone else, and by lunchtime, everyone was talking about it. Later, Maya found out Olivia hadn't cheated at all. The teacher had given her permission to retake part of the test. Maya felt terrible when she saw how upset Olivia was about the rumor.

What can you do instead?

- Ask yourself: *Would I say this if the person were standing right here?*

- Change the subject when others start gossiping.

- Say something positive about the person instead.

- Tell friends directly: "I don't feel comfortable talking about people when they're not here."

- Remember that keeping someone's secrets shows you're trustworthy.

Being the person who doesn't spread gossip or rumors might not always feel like the popular choice in the moment, but it shows your true character and makes you a friend people can really trust.

Conflict Resolution Steps

We will argue with our friends. We won't always agree with them, and sometimes, feelings might get hurt. Disagreements are a normal part of every friendship—even the very best ones! What matters isn't whether you have conflicts, but how you handle them when they happen.

When you find yourself in a disagreement with a friend, these steps can help you work through it in a healthy way:

1. **Cool down first:** If you're really upset, take some time to calm down before trying to fix things. Taking a few deep breaths or waiting until the next day can help you think more clearly.

2. **Talk face-to-face if possible:** It's easy to misunderstand texts or social media messages. If you can, have important conversations in person where you can see each other's facial expressions.

3. **Use "I feel" statements:** Instead of saying "You always leave me out," try "I feel sad when plans are made without me." This helps your friend understand your feelings without feeling attacked.

4. **Listen to understand, not to respond:** When your friend is talking, really try to understand their side instead of just thinking about what you'll say next.

5. **Look for compromise:** Is there a solution where both of you can get part of what you want? Maybe Sofia could suggest alternating weekends—one with just the original trio and the next including new friends.

6. **Apologize when needed:** If you realize you've done something hurtful, a sincere "I'm sorry" goes a long way. A good apology names what you did wrong and how you'll try to do better.

7. **Accept that some things change:** Sometimes resolving a conflict means accepting that your friendship is changing. This doesn't mean the friendship is over—just that it's growing in a new direction.

Remember, working through conflicts makes friendships stronger! When you practice these skills now, you're building relationship abilities that will help you throughout your whole life.

Being True to Yourself

You are you. You've got your own opinions and beliefs and things that make you happy. Sometimes, as friendships change, it can be tempting to change yourself, too. You might feel pressure to like what your friends like or agree with the most popular person in your group, even when you don't feel that way.

Being true to yourself means honoring your own feelings and values, even when they're different from your friends'. It means having the courage to stand up for what you believe is right, and being honest about the things you enjoy, even if they aren't considered "cool."

Understanding Your Values and Preferences

Before you can be true to yourself in friendships, you need to know what really matters to you. Your values are the ideas and beliefs that are most important to you—things like honesty, kindness, fairness, or creativity. Your preferences are the things you personally enjoy or care about, like your favorite activities, music, books, or ways to spend time.

When you're growing up, these values and preferences might change as you learn and experience new things. That's normal! The important thing is to notice what feels right to *you*, not just what others tell you to value.

Try asking yourself:

- *What three qualities do I most admire in other people?*

- *What activities make me lose track of time because I enjoy them so much?*

- *What would I stand up for, even if I had to stand alone?*

- *When do I feel most like "the real me"?*

Your answers to these questions can help you better understand your values and preferences.

Building Confidence to Express Your Genuine Opinions

Knowing what you think and feel is one thing—saying it out loud is another! Many girls worry about sharing their true opinions because they don't want to disagree with friends or stand out from the group. But sharing your authentic thoughts helps build stronger friendships in the long run.

Here's how to build confidence in expressing your genuine opinions:

- **Start small:** Practice sharing your preferences about simple things, like what movie you want to watch or what activity you'd enjoy. As this gets easier, you can work up to expressing opinions on more important matters.

- **Use "I" statements:** Saying "I really enjoy skating more than shopping" is easier for others to hear than "Shopping is boring."

- **Prepare for different reactions:** Sometimes friends will respect your opinion even if they disagree. Other times, they might try to change your mind or even tease you. Thinking ahead about how you'll respond helps you stay true to yourself.

- **Find your voice:** Everyone has their own style of expressing opinions. Some people are direct, while others are more gentle. Figure out what approach feels right for you while still getting your point across.

- **Remember that disagreement is okay:** True friends don't need to agree on everything. In fact, having different opinions can make friendships more interesting and help everyone learn new perspectives.

When Sofia finally talked to both Madison and Lily, she found the courage to share her real feelings. "I understand why Madison wants to include new friends sometimes," she said. "But I also value our special trio time like Lily does. Maybe we could do both?" By expressing her genuine opinion instead of just taking sides, Sofia stayed true to herself while also helping find a solution.

Being honest about your values and opinions isn't always easy, but it helps you build authentic friendships that accept the real you, not just who others want you to be.

Dealing With Peer Pressure in Friendships

Peer pressure happens when friends try to influence your choices or behaviors. Sometimes this pressure is obvious, like when someone directly says, "Come on, everyone's doing it!" Other times it's more subtle, like when you feel you need to dress a certain way to fit in, even though no one specifically told you to.

Not all peer pressure is bad. Friends might encourage you to try out for a team or study harder for a test. But when peer pressure pushes you to do things that make you uncomfortable or go against your values, it becomes a problem.

When you face peer pressure in your friendships, try these strategies:

- **Know your boundaries beforehand:** Think about your personal values and limits before you're in a tough situation. If you already know where you stand, it's easier to hold your ground.

- **Practice saying no confidently:** You don't need to make up complicated excuses. Simple responses like "No thanks, I don't want to" or "That's not really my thing" work well.

- **Suggest alternatives:** If friends are pushing for something you're not comfortable with, try suggesting a different activity: "I don't want to do that, but I'd be up for going to the park instead."

- **Use delay tactics when needed:** Saying "I need to ask my parents first" or "Let me think about it" can give you time to figure out how to respond.

- **Find strength in numbers:** Having even one friend who feels the same way you do can make it easier to resist pressure. Sometimes, others are just waiting for someone to speak up first.

- **Remember that real friends respect your choices:** If someone keeps pressuring you after you've clearly said no, that's not showing friendship.

Making New Friends Who Share Your Interests

As you discover more about yourself and your interests, you might find that you want to connect with people who share those interests. Making new friends doesn't mean replacing your old ones; it just means expanding your circle!

Here are ways to find and connect with new friends who share your interests:

- **Join clubs, teams, or groups related to things you enjoy:** Whether it's an art club, a soccer team, a coding class, or an environmental group, these activities naturally bring together people with similar interests.

- **Talk to people in your classes who seem to like similar things:** Did someone mention a book you love? Do they doodle amazing drawings in their notebook? These could be openings for conversation.

- **Be open about your interests:** Being authentic about what you enjoy makes it easier for like-minded people to find you. Wear that T-shirt with your favorite band, bring your book to read at lunch, or talk about the hobby you're passionate about.

- **Give people a chance:** Sometimes, you might have more in common with someone than you first realize. Try to look beyond cliques or first impressions.

- **Be patient:** Good friendships take time to develop. Start with small conversations and gradually build deeper connections.

Having different groups of friends for different parts of your life is completely normal and healthy! You might have school friends, neighborhood friends, and activity friends—all bringing different perspectives and experiences to your life.

When Sofia joined the school newspaper, she met Ellie, who shared her love of writing. This new friendship didn't replace her relationships with Lily and Madison; it just added another person who understood a different part of who Sofia was.

Ways to Maintain Your Identity Within a Friend Group

You can be a good friend but still be your own person. Many girls worry that having their own identity means being selfish or not caring about their friends. But that's not true at all! The strongest friendships happen when everyone feels free to be themselves.

Here are ways to stay true to yourself while still being part of a friend group:

- **Speak up about your preferences:** If the group always wants pizza but you're craving tacos, it's okay to suggest an alternative. Your opinion matters too!

- **Keep pursuing your personal interests:** If you love drawing but none of your friends do, that's fine! Keep taking art classes or sketching in your free time. You don't need to share every interest with your friends.

- **Take breaks when needed:** Sometimes you might need alone time or time with family, even when friends want to hang out. It's healthy to have different parts to your life.

- **Respectfully disagree when you have a different opinion:** You can say, "I see it differently" without making it into a big argument.

- **Choose your own style:** Maybe everyone in your group is wearing a certain brand or style, but you prefer something different. Wearing what makes you comfortable shows confidence.

- **Set boundaries around social media:** Don't feel pressured to post things just because your friends do, or to spend hours commenting on every post.

- **Remember that it's okay to have multiple friend groups:** Some girls connect with different friends for different activities or interests, and that's perfectly normal.

Sofia realized this when she started spending Tuesdays at art club while Madison had soccer and Lily had piano lessons. Having separate activities gave each of them something unique to bring back to their friendship: stories, skills, and new perspectives that made their time together even more interesting.

Being your own person within a friendship makes you a better friend. When you're honest about who you are and what you want, you create space for others to do the same. And that kind of authentic friendship is the kind that lasts, even as you all grow and change.

Continuing Sofia's Story

That Sunday afternoon, Sofia sprawled on her cousin Tessa's bed, watching her sort through her college textbooks. At seventeen, Tessa seemed so grown-up and confident. Sofia had always looked up to her.

"Something wrong, Sof? You've been sighing every five minutes," Tessa said, pushing aside a stack of notebooks.

Sofia picked at a loose thread on the comforter. "It's just friend stuff." Then, before she could talk herself out of it, she explained the whole situation with Lily and Madison.

"And they both keep texting me, asking whose side I'm on," Sofia finished. "I don't want to choose!"

Tessa nodded thoughtfully. "I had almost the exact same thing happen when I was your age. My friends Kayla and Jess got into this huge fight over who would be captain of our volleyball team."

"What did you do?" Sofia asked.

"I tried to make everyone happy by agreeing with whoever I was talking to at the time," Tessa admitted. "But that actually made everything worse, because they both figured out I was saying different things to each of them."

Sofia winced. "So what should I have done?"

"Honestly? The thing that finally worked was when I stopped trying to be in the middle and just told them both how I really felt," Tessa said. "Which was that I cared about both of them and didn't want to choose sides."

Sofia thought about this on the bus ride home. Maybe she needed to be honest with both Madison and Lily, even if they didn't like what she had to say.

The next day at school, Sofia took a deep breath and approached Madison at her locker before first period.

"Hey, can we talk for a minute?" Sofia asked.

Madison looked up from her phone. "Sure. Did you decide you're on my side about Saturday?"

"That's actually what I wanted to talk about," Sofia said, her heart pounding. "I don't want to take sides. You and Lily are both my friends."

Madison's face fell. "So, you're on her side."

"No," Sofia said firmly. "I'm not on anyone's side. I understand why you want to include other people sometimes. That makes sense to me. But I also get why Lily wants time with just us three."

"So, what are you saying?" Madison asked, crossing her arms.

"I'm saying I want to be friends with both of you, and I wish you two could work this out. But if you can't, I'm still not going to choose."

Madison was quiet for a moment. "I guess that's... fair," she finally said, though she didn't look thrilled.

At lunch, Sofia had a similar conversation with Lily, who also seemed disappointed but eventually nodded.

"I still think Madison is being unfair," Lily said. "But I get that you don't want to be in the middle."

The next few weeks weren't perfect. Sometimes Sofia hung out with just Lily, sometimes with Madison and her new friends. Occasionally, all three of them spent time together, though it felt different than before.

One afternoon, as Sofia walked home with both girls after a study session, she realized something important. Their friendship was changing, but maybe that wasn't all bad. Madison seemed happier now that she could spend time with different groups, and Lily was starting to open up to some of the new girls, too.

Sofia had worried that growing up meant growing apart. But now she wondered if maybe it just meant growing in new directions—still connected, but with more branches, like a tree that gets fuller and stronger over time.

That night, Sofia wrote in her journal:

Today I realized that being true to myself doesn't mean I have to lose my friends. It just means our friendship might look different than before. And different doesn't have to mean worse.

As she closed her journal, Sofia felt a new kind of confidence. Standing up for herself hadn't been easy, but it had been worth it. For the first time in weeks, she fell asleep without worrying about tomorrow's friendship drama.

Self-Reflection Section

My Friendship Values Worksheet

Circle the five qualities that are most important to you in a friend:

- honesty

- kindness

- loyalty

- sense of humor

- being a good listener

- respectful of differences

- trustworthiness

- supportiveness

- similar interests

- forgiveness

- understanding

- fun to be around

My ideal friend would:

_____

_____

_____

_____

I want to be the kind of friend who:

_____

_____

_____

Journal Prompts

- *When do I feel most comfortable and accepted in my friendships?*

- *What's one way I've changed as a friend in the past year?*

- *If I could improve one thing about how I am as a friend, what would it be?*

- *How do I handle it when a friend and I disagree?*

- *What makes me feel valued in a friendship?*

Sofia's Reflection

What I value most in friendships: *honesty, kindness, understanding, trustworthiness, being a good listener*

My ideal friend would: *accept me for who I am, tell me the truth even when it's hard, listen without judging, understand that I have other friends too, make me laugh when I'm feeling down*

I want to be the kind of friend who: *stays true to myself while still being supportive, doesn't gossip or spread rumors, makes everyone feel included when possible, is honest without being hurtful, respects different opinions*

What I learned from my friendship challenge: *I learned that I don't have to choose sides or be in the middle of conflicts. I can care about both friends while still setting boundaries. I also learned that friendships can change* *without ending, and that being honest about how I feel usually works out better than trying to please everyone.*

Friendship Inventory

Think about your current friendships and check all that apply:

☐ I can be myself around my friends.

☐ I feel pressured to agree with my friends even when I don't.

☐ My friends respect when I say no to something.

☐ I've changed parts of myself to fit in with my friends.

☐ I have different friends for different interests or activities.

☐ I worry about losing friends if I don't do what they want.

☐ My friends accept me even when we disagree.

☐ I feel drained after spending time with certain friends.

Balancing Friendships and Personal Needs

- *What's one boundary I could set to better honor my own needs?*

- *How can I make time for my personal interests while maintaining friendships?*

- *What's a kind way to tell a friend when I need space?*

- *How do I want to handle situations where friends are pressuring me?*

Remember that healthy friendships have room for everyone to be themselves. As you grow and change, your friendships will too—and that's perfectly normal!

CHAPTER 6: BODY CONFIDENCE AND SELF-LOVE

Emily stood in front of her bedroom mirror, frowning. Her jeans felt tighter around her hips and thighs than last month.

"Emily! The bus will be here in ten minutes!" her dad called.

"Coming!" she shouted, though she stayed put. She turned sideways, studying her profile. Was that a little belly poking out? She sucked in her stomach, holding her breath until her face turned red.

With a sigh, Emily pulled off the jeans and tossed them onto the pile of discarded outfits. The leggings were too tight, the jeans too stiff, and her favorite skirt now clung to her new curves.

She finally settled on an oversized sweatshirt over different jeans, despite the warm weather. At least it covered everything.

As she packed her homework, Emily noticed the magazine with a teenage pop star on the cover. The girl looked perfect— flat stomach, long legs, smooth skin. Emily touched the small pimple on her chin. Why couldn't she look like that?

At school, Emily noticed her friends' bodies seemed different from hers. Zoe was slender with delicate wrists. Kaitlyn was taller but hadn't changed shape much. Why was Emily the only one changing in these uncomfortable ways?

In PE class, when Emily reached for her toes, her gym shirt rode up, exposing her stomach.

"Looks like someone's been eating too many cookies," Tyler commented as he walked past.

Heat rushed to Emily's face as she quickly tugged her shirt down. It was just a stupid joke, but it felt like he had seen right through to her insecurities.

That evening, Emily examined her changing body in the mirror—the new curve of her hips, slight swell of her chest, roundness of her cheeks.

Emily knew these changes were normal from health class. But knowing something and feeling okay about it were different things.

As she went to bed, she wondered if she would ever feel comfortable in this new body that seemed to be changing without her permission.

Accepting Your Changing Body

You have this body, this body that moves, breathes, and lives for you. This body that allows you to do stuff with your friends and family, that allows you to enjoy all your favorite foods and laugh like there's no tomorrow. All of that is pretty amazing when you think about it!

During puberty, your body goes through many changes. These changes might sometimes feel confusing or even uncomfortable, like they did for Emily. You might grow taller, your hips might get wider, you might develop breasts, and you might notice more curves than you had before. You might also notice your skin changing, with pimples appearing where your skin was always clear before.

All of these changes are completely normal. They're your body's way of growing up, and they happen to everyone (yes, everyone!), though they might happen at different times and in different ways for each person.

Some girls start developing curves and breasts as early as 8 or 9 years old, while others might not notice these changes until they're 12, 13, or even later. Some girls grow tall very quickly, while others grow more slowly over a longer period of time.

Some girls develop more noticeable curves, while others have more straight-up-and-down body types.

This wide range of normal development is why it can be so confusing when you compare yourself to friends your own age. Your friend might already have started developing breasts while you haven't, or you might be the one developing first. Neither of you is "wrong" or "behind" or "ahead." You're both just following your own body's unique timeline.

Your body shape and development schedule are influenced by many factors that you can't control, including:

- your genes (the traits you inherit from your family)

- your natural body type

- your hormones (those chemical messengers that trigger puberty changes)

- even things like nutrition and overall health

Looking at magazines, movies, or social media might make you think there's only one "right" way for a body to look. But those images don't show the reality of normal, healthy bodies. In fact, many of those images aren't even real!

Most photos you see in magazines or online have been changed using computer programs. Photographers and editors can

- make people look taller or shorter.

- remove any pimples, scars, or blemishes.

- make body parts look bigger or smaller.

- change the color of skin, hair, and eyes.

- even change the shape of someone's body completely!

Even some of your "everyday" photos your friends might post are carefully posed, taken from certain angles, or filtered to look a specific way.

Real bodies, bodies that are healthy, normal, wonderful bodies, come in all shapes and sizes. So, it's okay to have wider hips or broader shoulders. Instead of focusing on how your body looks, try to appreciate what it can do.

How to Handle Comments About Your Body From Others

Sometimes, people have no boundaries, and they say whatever, whenever, in whichever way, without fully thinking about the consequences of their words. This is especially true when it comes to comments about bodies. Friends and family will likely make remarks about your height, your weight, your skin, or the ways your body is changing—and these comments can stick with you even when the person who said them has forgotten all about it.

When someone makes a comment about your body, remember this:

- Their comment says more about them than it does about you.

- You don't have to accept their opinion as truth.

- You have the right to set boundaries about body talk.

Here are some ways to handle different types of body comments:

Unexpected Comments From Classmates or Friends

- Use a calm, confident voice to say, "I'm not comfortable with comments about my body."

- Change the subject to something completely different.

- Ask simply "Why would you say that?" (This often makes people realize they've crossed a line.)

- Use humor to deflect if that feels right to you.

Well-Meaning but Hurtful Comments From Family Members

- Explain how the comment makes you feel: "When you comment on my weight, it makes me feel self-conscious."

- Set a clear boundary: "I'd prefer if we didn't discuss my body changes."

- Suggest alternative ways they can support you: "Instead of commenting on how I look, I'd love to hear that you're proud of how hard I worked on my science project."

Comments From Adults in Authority (Like Coaches or Teachers)

- If the comment is about your health or safety, try to listen objectively.

- If the comment feels inappropriate or makes you uncomfortable, tell a parent or another trusted adult.

- Remember that even adults don't always know the right thing to say about growing bodies.

Comments on Social Media

- Remember that you can delete negative comments on your own posts.

- Block or restrict people who make hurtful body comments.

- Consider taking a break from social media if body comments are affecting you.

Most importantly, build up your own inner voice to be stronger than outside comments. When you hear something negative about your body, counter it in your mind with something positive: *My body is strong*, *My body is exactly where it needs to be right now*, or *My worth isn't determined by how I look*.

And remember, while it might be tempting to comment on others' bodies in what seems like a positive way ("You look so skinny!" or "I wish I had your curves!"). Even these comments can make people uncomfortable. We're all trying to focus less on how bodies look and more on what amazing things they can do!

When Body Concerns Need Extra Support

Sometimes body image struggles go beyond occasional negative thoughts and become more serious concerns that need adult support. It's important to know the difference between normal body consciousness and issues that might need help from a trusted grown-up.

Consider talking to an adult if

- you're constantly thinking about your body in negative ways.

- you're avoiding activities you used to enjoy because of body concerns.

- you're changing your eating habits dramatically to try to change your body.

- you feel sad or anxious about your body most days.

- you're exercising excessively to try to change your shape.

- you find yourself comparing your body to others' all the time.

- physical changes are causing you pain or severe discomfort.

There's nothing wrong with asking for help! Talking to a parent, school nurse, counselor, or doctor about body concerns isn't a sign of weakness; it's a sign of strength and self-awareness.

Finding Body-Positive Role Models

The people we look up to can strongly influence how we feel about our own bodies. Surrounding yourself with body-positive influences can help you develop a healthier relationship with your changing body.

Look for role models who do the following:

- focus on what their bodies can do rather than just how they look

- represent diverse body types, shapes, and sizes

- talk about bodies with respect and appreciation

- demonstrate confidence regardless of whether they match societal "ideals"

- show that success and happiness don't depend on appearance

These role models can be:

- family members who have a healthy relationship with their bodies

- athletes who celebrate strength and ability

- artists or musicians who express themselves confidently

- actors or public figures who advocate for body acceptance

- book characters who are valued for their character, not appearance

- friends who lift others up instead of comparing or criticizing

You can also seek out body-positive content online and in books. Many authors, artists, and content creators are working to spread messages of body acceptance and appreciation for all body types. Filling your feed with diverse, positive images and messages can help counter the unrealistic standards often shown in mainstream media.

Remember that becoming a body-positive person yourself makes you a role model for others, too! When you speak kindly about your own body and avoid criticizing others', you help create a more accepting environment for everyone.

Building Confidence From the Inside Out

True confidence doesn't come from looking a certain way. It grows from appreciating yourself from the inside out. When you build inner confidence, you'll find that how you feel about your body can improve too.

The Connection Between How We Treat Our Bodies and How We Feel About Them

Have you ever noticed that how you treat your body affects how you feel about it? This connection works in both directions:

When we respect and are kind to our bodies, we tend to feel better about them. And when we feel good about our bodies, we're more likely to take good care of them. It creates a positive cycle that builds confidence from the inside out.

If you constantly say negative things about your body, you'll probably start to believe those negative thoughts. But if you treat your body like something valuable and worthy of care, your feelings often follow.

Here are ways to create this positive connection:

- **Move your body in ways that feel good:** When you dance, swim, bike, or play sports that you enjoy, you start to appreciate what your body can DO instead of just how it LOOKS. You might find yourself thinking, *Wow, my legs are really strong!* instead of worrying about their shape.

- **Feed your body with care:** Eating nutritious foods most of the time (while still enjoying treats!) gives you energy and helps your body work at its best. Notice how different foods make you feel, not just how they might affect your appearance. When you eat to nourish yourself rather than to change your shape, you develop a healthier relationship with both food and your body.

- **Rest when you need it:** Getting enough sleep and taking breaks when you're tired shows respect for your body's needs. It's like telling your body, "I'm listening to you and I care about what you need."

- **Speak kindly about your body:** Even if you don't always feel positive about your appearance, try to avoid harsh criticism. When you catch yourself thinking something negative, try to replace it with a neutral or positive thought. Instead of *I hate my stomach*, try *This is just how my body is shaped* or *My body helps me do things I enjoy*.

- **Dress in ways that make you feel good:** Wear clothes that fit comfortably and that you like, rather than hiding your body or trying to change how it looks. When you're comfortable in your clothes, you're more likely to feel comfortable in your skin.

When you start treating your body with kindness and respect, you teach yourself to appreciate it more, even if it doesn't match society's narrow beauty standards. This appreciation builds genuine confidence—the kind that comes from knowing your worth isn't determined by your appearance.

Remember that building this kind of confidence takes time, especially during puberty when your body is changing rapidly. Be patient with yourself, and know that the effort you put into developing a positive relationship with your body now will benefit you for your entire life.

How to Practice Genuine Self-Care and Self-Kindness

Self-care, the kind that goes beyond bubble baths and face masks (though those can be nice, too!), is about treating yourself with the same kindness and understanding you would offer to a good friend. It's about making choices that support your overall wellbeing—not just in the moment, but in the long run, too.

Here's how to practice genuine self-care and self-kindness:

- **Listen to your body's signals:** Your body sends you messages all day long. Are you hungry? Tired? Need to stretch? Learning to notice and respond to these signals is a fundamental form of self-care. Rest when you're tired, eat when you're hungry, and move when you feel restless.

- **Speak to yourself kindly:** Pay attention to your inner voice. Would you talk to a friend the way you talk to yourself? If not, try to shift your self-talk to be more understanding and supportive. Instead of "I look awful today," try "I'm having a tough day, but that's okay."

- **Set healthy boundaries:** It's okay to say no to activities that drain you or people who make you feel bad about yourself. Standing up for your needs is an important form of self-kindness.

- **Find joy in small things:** Notice and appreciate little pleasures throughout your day: the warmth of sunshine, a favorite song, a moment of laughter with friends. This helps build resilience and positive feelings.

- **Create a comfort kit:** Collect items that help you feel better when you're having a hard day: maybe a favorite book, a soft blanket, pictures of happy memories, or a playlist of uplifting songs. Turn to these when you need a boost.

- **Practice forgiveness—especially with yourself:** Everyone makes mistakes or has bad days. Learning to forgive yourself when things don't go perfectly is a powerful form of self-kindness.

- **Connect with supportive people:** Spending time with friends and family who make you feel good about yourself is essential self-care. These people remind you of your worth beyond appearance.

- **Do things just because they make you happy:** Whether it's drawing, playing with your pet, or watching your favorite show, make time for activities that bring you joy, with no pressure to be productive or perfect.

Remember that self-care isn't selfish. Taking care of yourself gives you the energy and emotional resources to be your best self and to care for others, too. When you treat yourself with kindness and respect, you also set an example for how others should treat you.

How you care for yourself during these years of change will help shape your relationship with yourself for years to come. Small acts of self-kindness add up over time, helping you build a foundation of self-respect and confidence that goes much deeper than appearance.

Continuing Emily's Story

A week later, Emily sat with her visiting Aunt Jenna at the kitchen table, pushing cereal around her bowl.

"Something on your mind?" Aunt Jenna asked.

Emily hesitated, then asked, "When you were my age, did you ever feel weird about how you looked?"

Aunt Jenna laughed. "Only every day for about three years straight!"

Emily told her everything—the tight jeans, the magazines, Tyler's comment, the constant comparisons.

"It's like I'm constantly judging myself," Emily finished. "And the voice in my head is super mean."

"Ah, that voice," Aunt Jenna nodded. "Here's something I wish someone had told me: you don't have to believe everything you think. Those thoughts about your body being wrong? They're just thoughts, not facts."

Aunt Jenna suggested Emily imagine what she'd say to a friend with similar feelings. Would she agree they looked terrible? Or would she be kind?

Over the next days, Emily noticed how often she criticized herself. She started practicing more compassionate self-talk.

That Saturday, Emily's mom took her shopping for clothes that actually fit her changing body. A pair of stretchy jeans felt comfortable around her new curves. A colorful t-shirt made her smile.

In science class, Ms. Rodriguez described bodies as "incredible machines" that perform thousands of complex functions. Emily had never thought about her body that way before.

She rediscovered bike riding and felt grateful for her strong legs while pedaling up a steep hill. Who cared what they looked like in shorts?

Emily also noticed that even the "perfect" eighth-grade girls complained about their appearances. Maybe nobody felt completely confident about their looks.

That night, Emily looked at herself with curiosity and kindness instead of criticism. She saw her dad's eyes, strong arms that could carry her brother, and a healthy body working exactly as it should.

"You're doing just fine," she whispered to her reflection.

Emily made a list titled "Cool Things My Body Can Do," realizing she'd been so focused on appearance that she'd forgotten all the amazing things her body could do.

She still had self-conscious days, but now had tools to shift her thinking—acknowledging negative thoughts without believing them, and focusing instead on what her body could do, not just how it looked.

Self-Reflection Section

Three Things I Love About Myself

Just like Emily made her list, you can too! These can be about your appearance, your abilities, your personality—anything that makes you.

1. _____

2. _____

3. _____

Journal Prompts

Use these questions to explore your thoughts about body image:

- *When do I feel most comfortable in my body?*

- *Who makes me feel good about myself?*

- *What activities make me appreciate what my body can do?*

- *How do I feel after looking at social media or magazines?*

- *What's one way my body has helped me do something I enjoy?*

My Personal Strengths

List your strengths that have nothing to do with appearance:

Things I'm good at:

_____

_____

_____

_____

Character traits I value in myself:

_____

_____

_____

_____

Emily's Reflection

Three things I love about myself:

1. *My eyes. They're dark brown like my dad's and show my feelings.*

2. *My strong legs that can ride my bike up big hills.*

3. *My creative mind that comes up with good ideas for art projects.*

When do I feel most comfortable in my body?

When I'm playing basketball or riding my bike, I stop thinking about how I look and just enjoy what I'm doing.

Who makes me feel good about myself?

Aunt Jenna always makes me feel like I'm enough just as I am. And my friend Zoe never talks about people's appearances in a negative way.

What activities make me appreciate what my body can do?

Playing sports, dancing in my room to favorite songs, and carrying my little brother when he's tired.

Media Reality Check

Use these questions when looking at images in media:

- *Has this image been edited or filtered?*

- *Are they using special lighting or camera angles?*

- *Is this person posed in a way that real people don't usually stand or sit?*

- *Could I find ten different body types in this magazine/show/website?*

- *Does this image make me feel good or bad about myself?*

Changing the Conversation in Your Head

When you catch yourself thinking negative thoughts, try these alternatives:

- Instead of: *I hate how my stomach looks.*

  - Try thinking: *This is just how bodies are shaped. My body helps me do things I love.*

- Instead of: *Everyone looks better than me.*

  - Try thinking: *Everyone is different, and that's what makes people interesting.*

- Instead of: *I need to lose weight.*

  - Try thinking: *My body is growing and changing just as it should be.*

- Instead of: *My skin looks awful.*

    - Try thinking: *Almost everyone gets pimples during puberty. They'll clear up.*

- Instead of: *My thighs are too big.*

    - Try thinking: *My legs are strong and help me run, jump, and play.*

Remember, changing how you talk to yourself takes practice. Be patient with yourself and celebrate small moments when you catch a negative thought and turn it around!

Chapter 7:

Standing Up for Yourself—

Knowing Your Worth

Ava was excited when popular Zoe invited her to a sleepover, hoping to finally fit in at her new school after three months. Her mom reminded her to call if needed before dropping her off.

At first, the sleepover was everything Ava hoped—pizza, music, and casual conversation with Zoe and four other girls in the decorated basement. Ava began to relax, feeling like she belonged.

But after Zoe's parents went to bed, the mood shifted. Zoe revealed her real plan: sneaking out at midnight to meet boys at the park. Everyone else seemed thrilled, but Ava felt uncomfortable.

"Won't the alarm go off?" Ava asked, trying to sound practical rather than scared.

"My parents never set it," Zoe replied with an eye roll. "They sleep like rocks anyway."

When Ava hesitated, Zoe's tone changed: "Don't be such a baby!"

"Yeah, don't ruin it for everyone," added Mackenzie, whom Ava had just met.

Feeling pressured, Ava reluctantly agreed despite her internal objections. While the others excitedly discussed the boys, she slipped away to the bathroom and texted her mom: "Not feeling great. Could you pick me up early? Say it's a family thing?"

Her mom responded immediately: "Everything ok? I can be there in 15."

When Zoe's mom announced her mother's arrival, Ava gathered her things. Zoe looked suspicious: "Family emergency on a Friday night? You're just scared about tonight, aren't you?"

In the car, her mom asked if she wanted to talk.

"Not really," Ava replied, staring out the window.

As they drove home, Ava felt conflicted. She was relieved to be safe but disappointed in herself. Why couldn't she have just told Zoe directly that she wasn't comfortable? Why make up an excuse instead of standing her ground?

Ava realized she couldn't keep running away when pressured. There had to be a better way to handle these situations—a way that let her be true to herself without needing escape plans and excuses.

What Is Body Autonomy?

Body autonomy means you have the right to make decisions about your own body. It's the understanding that your body belongs to you, and you get to decide what happens to it, who touches it, and what you do with it.

Think of your body like your bedroom—a space that's yours where you get to decide who comes in and what happens there. Just like you wouldn't want someone barging into your room without permission or rearranging your things without asking, you deserve the same respect for your body.

Body autonomy includes lots of different things:

- deciding who can hug you or touch you

- choosing what activities feel safe and comfortable

- setting boundaries about personal space

- making choices about your appearance

- speaking up when something doesn't feel right

As you grow up, you'll get more and more control over decisions about your body. When you were little, grown-ups made most decisions for you. Now that you're older, you get more say, though parents and doctors still help with important health decisions.

Understanding body autonomy helps you respect yourself *and* others. Just as you have the right to control what happens to your body, everyone else has that same right. That's why we ask before hugging someone or borrowing their things.

Having body autonomy doesn't mean you can do whatever you want without thinking about safety or rules. It means you have the right to speak up about your comfort and boundaries, and others should listen and respect those boundaries.

Setting Boundaries With Confidence

Boundaries are how we let other people know what we're willing and not willing to tolerate. They are how we show others what's okay and what's not okay when they interact with us. If you want a more tangible example, picture a big invisible bubble wrapped around you. This boundary serves to protect your feelings, your personal space, and your choices. When someone crosses your boundary, it can feel uncomfortable or even upsetting; that's usually a sign you need to speak up!

Some boundaries are physical (like not wanting to be tickled), while others are about your feelings (like not wanting to be teased about certain topics). Everyone has different boundaries, and that's perfectly normal. What feels okay to one person might not feel okay to you—and that's fine!

Practical Strategies for Identifying Personal Boundaries

Recognizing the "Uncomfortable Feeling" as a Boundary Signal

Your body is amazing at telling you when something doesn't feel right! Pay attention to physical clues that might signal a boundary is being crossed:

- feeling unsettled in your stomach

- wanting to step back or create distance

- feeling your face get hot

- tension in your shoulders or chest

- the urge to cross your arms

- feeling suddenly quiet or unable to speak up

These feelings are like your body's alarm system, telling you, "Hey, something's not right here!" When you notice these feelings, it's a sign that one of your boundaries might need protecting.

Different Types of Boundaries

Physical Boundaries

These are about your body and personal space:

- how close people stand to you

- who can touch you and how

- whether you want to give hugs, high-fives, or no contact

- having privacy when changing clothes or using the bathroom

Emotional Boundaries

These involve your feelings and inner thoughts:

- what personal information you share with others

- how people speak to you and treat you

- which topics feel too private to discuss

- how much emotional support you can give others

Social Boundaries

These relate to your social life and time:

- who you spend time with

- what activities you participate in

- how much time you need for yourself

- what behavior is okay in your friendships

How Boundaries Might Change in Different Situations

Just like you might wear different clothes depending on the weather, your boundaries might change depending on the situation or the people involved:

- You might be okay with a family member hugging you, but prefer a high-five from a classmate.

- You might share personal feelings with close friends but keep conversations more general with acquaintances.

- You might have stricter boundaries when you're tired or not feeling well.

- Your boundaries today might be different than they were a year ago.

It's perfectly normal for your boundaries to shift and change as you grow!

Identifying Your Non-Negotiables vs. Flexible Boundaries

Some boundaries are firm and shouldn't be crossed no matter what. We call these your "non-negotiable boundaries." Others might be a little more flexible, depending on the context, environment, and situation that you're in.

Non-Negotiable Boundaries

- No one should touch your private body parts (except doctors with a parent present for health reasons).

- No one should pressure you to do things that make you feel unsafe.

- No one should call you mean names or bully you.

- No one should take or look through your personal things without permission.

Flexible Boundaries

These often change based on your comfort level:

- whether you're in the mood for physical games like tag or wrestling

- what topics you're comfortable talking about with different people

- how much alone time you need on different days

- how much help you want with various tasks

Take some time to think about your own boundaries. What makes you feel uncomfortable? What situations always feel okay? The better you understand your own boundaries, the easier it becomes to communicate them to others!

Saying No and Meaning It

Saying no can be really hard because we grow up being told that being "good" means being helpful, agreeable, and putting other people's needs before our own. We worry that saying no might

- make someone not like us anymore.

- seem mean or selfish.

- hurt someone's feelings.

- make us look like we're not being a team player.

- cause someone to get angry with us.

This can make saying no feel scary, even when we know we should!

The Difference Between Being Nice and Being a Pushover

Being nice is about treating others with kindness and respect. Being a pushover is allowing people to make choices for you, even when those choices make you uncomfortable.

You can be a kind, caring person *and* still say no when something doesn't feel right. In fact, having clear boundaries actually helps your relationships because

- people know what to expect from you.

- you avoid feeling secretly resentful.

- you have more energy for the things you truly want to do.

- your yes becomes more meaningful because it's honest.

Remember: Real friends will respect your no and still like you!

How to Overcome People-Pleasing Tendencies

If you often find yourself saying yes when you really want to say no, try these tips:

- **Practice saying no in small, low-pressure situations:** Try it first with safe people like family members: "No thanks, I don't want another helping" or "I'd rather not watch that movie."

- **Buy yourself some time:** When someone asks you to do something, it's okay to say, "Let me think about it and get back to you." This gives you space to decide how you really feel.

- **Have some ready-made phrases:**

    - "Thanks for asking, but I can't."

    - "That doesn't work for me."

    - "I'm not comfortable with that."

    - "I need to say no this time."

- **Remember that a reason is not always needed:** You don't always have to explain why you're saying no. A simple, kind no is enough.

- **Think about future-you:** When tempted to say yes just to please someone, ask yourself: *How will I feel about this later? Will I regret saying yes?*

- **Start with "I" statements:** Saying "I don't want to" or "I'm not comfortable with that" is stronger than "I can't" or "I'm not allowed to."

- **Practice in the mirror:** It might feel silly, but practicing saying no with a firm voice and confident posture can help when the real situation comes up.

Remember that saying no gets easier with practice! Each time you stand up for your boundaries, you're building an important skill that will serve you throughout your entire life.

Dealing With Guilt After Setting Boundaries

If you ever feel guilty after having set a boundary, I want you to remember that if you never learn how to stand up for yourself and advocate for your needs, you'll find yourself in situations you don't really want to be in. The guilt is part and parcel of healthy boundary setting. Yes, you'll worry that you've hurt someone's feelings or that they might be upset with you, but that doesn't mean that you've done something wrong; they're just a sign that you're learning a new skill.

Here are some ways to handle those guilty feelings:

- **Remind yourself why boundaries matter:** You're doing this because you want to feel more at home in your life, in your body, in your choices that you make. This is not selfish—it's necessary!

- **Notice the difference between guilt and discomfort:** Sometimes, what feels like guilt is actually just the discomfort of trying something new. Like learning any new skill, setting boundaries feels awkward at first, but it gets easier with practice.

- **Talk to someone supportive:** Share your feelings with a parent, older sibling, or another trusted person who understands the importance of boundaries.

- **Remember that how others respond is their responsibility:** You can set a boundary kindly and clearly, but you can't control how others react to it. Their disappointment or frustration is not your fault.

- **Think about what you would tell a friend:** If your friend told you they felt guilty for setting a boundary, what would you say to them? Try giving yourself that same understanding and encouragement.

The more you practice setting healthy boundaries, the more natural it will feel. Eventually, you'll recognize that taking care of yourself allows you to be more genuinely present and helpful in your relationships, rather than doing things out of guilt or pressure.

Continuing Ava's Story

The morning after the sleepover, Ava avoided checking the group texts, feeling conflicted about her escape tactic.

"Who died in your cereal?" her older sister Mia asked, entering the kitchen.

Ava explained everything—the midnight plan, her discomfort, and her escape strategy.

"Instead of telling them I wasn't comfortable, I just ran away," Ava concluded. "Now I don't know what to say at school."

"Speaking up can be really hard," Mia sympathized, sharing her own middle school experience of lying about a dentist appointment rather than refusing to skip school.

"What happened?" Ava asked.

"They found out I lied, which was worse than being honest," Mia admitted. "But in high school, my health teacher taught us about boundaries. Real friends respect your 'no.'"

Mia suggested they practice responses, role-playing as Zoe: "Come on, Ava, don't be such a baby! We're all sneaking out!"

After several attempts, Ava found her voice: "I'm not comfortable with that plan. I don't think it's a good idea to sneak out."

"The key is being clear and confident," Mia explained. "You don't need to apologize for having boundaries."

"But what if they stop being my friends?" Ava worried.

"Then they weren't very good friends to begin with," Mia replied.

On Monday, Zoe confronted Ava: "Well, look who it is. Miss Family Emergency."

Taking a deep breath, Ava asked to talk privately and confessed: "I wasn't honest Friday night. I just wasn't comfortable with sneaking out and didn't know how to say that."

To her surprise, Zoe shrugged. "Whatever. We didn't end up going anyway. My dad woke up around midnight."

"Next time, just say you don't want to do something. It's not a big deal," Zoe added.

Over the following weeks, Ava noticed that clearly stating her boundaries caused some friends to drift away, while others respected her more. She connected with different classmates who shared her values, joining the school newspaper where she met Elena.

When Elena mentioned a party with potential alcohol, she suggested a movie night instead.

Ava smiled, realizing that standing up for herself hadn't led to social disaster. Instead, it had helped her find people who respected her values and made her comfortable being herself, which felt much better than fitting in with people who didn't respect her boundaries.

Your Time to Reflect

My Personal Boundaries Worksheet

Physical Boundaries
These are about your body, personal space, and physical comfort.

I'm comfortable with:

_____

_____

_____

I'm not *comfortable with:*

_____

_____

_____

Emotional Boundaries

These are about your feelings, privacy, and emotional comfort.

I'm comfortable with:

_____

_____

_____

I'm not *comfortable with:*

_____

_____

_____

Social Boundaries

These are about your time, activities, and social comfort.

I'm comfortable with:

_____

_____

I'm not comfortable with:

_____

_____

When It's Hard to Say No

Think about times when saying no feels especially difficult:

- With which people is it hardest to set boundaries?

- In what situations do you find yourself agreeing when you don't want to?

- What are you afraid might happen if you say no?

- What has happened in the past when you've tried to set a boundary?

_____

_____

_____

_____

Practice Your Boundary Statements

For each situation, write a clear, confident boundary statement.

When someone asks to copy your homework:

_____

When someone pressures you to do something unsafe:

_____

When someone teases you in a way that hurts your feelings:

_____

When you need some alone time:

_____

Ava's Reflection

Situations where it's hard for me to say no:

- _when popular kids invite me to do things_

- _when someone might think I'm not fun_

- _when I'm the only one who doesn't want to do something_

- _when I'm afraid of losing friends_

My boundary statements that I'm practicing:

- "I'm not comfortable with that plan."

- "No, I don't want to do that, but thanks for asking."

- "That doesn't work for me. I need to go home now."

What I've learned:

I've realized that real friends should respect my boundaries. When I'm clear about what I'm comfortable with, I actually feel more confident. I don't need to make up excuses—I can just be honest about how I feel.

Confidence-Building Affirmations

Circle the affirmations that resonate with you or write your own:

- "My feelings and boundaries matter."

- "I can be kind *and* set limits."

- "Saying no to things that don't feel right is brave."

- "I deserve to be respected."

- "Real friends accept me for who I am."

- "My body belongs to me."

- "I trust my instincts about what feels right and wrong."

- "Setting boundaries shows self-respect."

- "I can say no and still be a good person."

My personal affirmation:

_____

_____

Remember that setting boundaries takes practice. Be patient with yourself as you learn this important skill!

CHAPTER 8: NAVIGATING THE JOURNEY OF GROWING UP

L ily sat on her bedroom floor surrounded by photo albums. Tasked with selecting photos for a family slideshow, she became engrossed in the chronicle of her own life.

"I can't believe how little I was," she murmured, touching a photo of her five-year-old self in a princess costume. She had been so confident then about becoming an astronaut-ballerina-veterinarian.

Now, at eleven, the future felt both closer and more confusing. Recent photos showed how much she'd changed in just one year—taller, with a thinner face and more grown-up smile.

"Find any good ones?" Mom asked, joining her.

"Yeah, a few," Lily answered.

Mom picked up a baby photo. "You were such a serious baby. Now look at you—almost a middle schooler."

"Don't remind me," Lily groaned, smiling nonetheless.

Dad appeared, and they talked about middle school, with parents explaining the challenges ahead: six different teachers, tracking assignments, and tricky locker combinations.

"That sounds like a lot to handle," Lily worried.

"You'll be ready," Mom assured her. "You're becoming more responsible every day."

Yet that evening, Lily realized she'd forgotten to email her science teacher about a missing assignment. How would she manage six teachers when she could barely keep track of four?

The next day, Ms. Richards announced a writing assignment: "Write about what you want to be when you grow up."

While her classmates immediately began writing—Zach about becoming a video game designer, Emma about becoming a doctor—Lily stared at her blank paper. When she was younger, the answer had been easy. Now she had no idea.

She eventually wrote vague sentences about "helping people" and "doing something important," but her heart wasn't in it. How could she know what she wanted to be when she didn't even know who she was becoming?

That night, Lily stared at the glow-in-the-dark stars on her ceiling. Her stuffed animals had been relocated to make room for "more grown-up" throw pillows.

Everyone expected her to know what she was doing, be excited about growing up, and have everything figured out.

But what if she didn't? What if she wasn't ready? What if everyone else knew exactly who they wanted to be, while she was still trying to figure out who she was right now?

Lily hugged her pillow close, wondering if she was the only one who felt caught between—not quite a little kid anymore, but definitely not ready to have her whole future planned out. Growing up was happening whether she was ready or not, and that thought was both exciting and terrifying all at once.

What Does Growing Up Mean?

Have you ever noticed how adults sometimes smile when kids say, "I can't wait to grow up"? That's because growing up isn't something that happens with many small steps along the way.

Growing is when you change from a child who needs lots of help into a teenager and then an adult who can take care of themselves and others. But this doesn't happen overnight! Just like how your body changes little by little during puberty, your abilities, responsibilities, and independence also grow bit by bit.

When you were very young, adults did almost everything for you—they chose your clothes, prepared your food, and made most decisions. Now that you're older, you probably pick out your own clothes, maybe make simple meals, and have more say in decisions that affect you. That's growing up in action!

As you continue to grow, bit by bit, you will learn

- to make more decisions on your own.

- to take care of more personal responsibilities.

- to develop your own opinions and values.

- to figure out who you are and what matters to you.

- from mistakes and solve problems.

- to consider how your actions affect others.

Some parts of growing up are exciting—like staying up later, having more privacy, or gaining new privileges. Other parts might feel challenging—like having more homework, dealing with complicated friendships, or being expected to control your emotions better.

Growing up doesn't mean leaving behind all the things you enjoyed as a younger child. Many adults still love playing games, watching cartoons, or collecting things they enjoyed when they were young. Growing up means adding new interests and abilities while still appreciating parts of your younger self.

Remember that everyone grows up at their own pace. You might feel more mature than some of your friends in certain ways, while they might seem more grown-up in others. That's completely normal! The important thing is to embrace each step of your own journey.

The Balance Between Freedom and Accountability

As you grow up, you'll notice something interesting happens: The more freedom you get, the more accountability comes with it. Freedom and accountability are like two sides of the same coin—they go together.

Freedom means having more choices and independence. It's being able to decide things for yourself, like how to spend your time, who to be friends with, or how to express yourself. Freedom feels good because it gives you control over your own life.

Accountability means being responsible for your choices and actions. It's understanding that what you do affects both yourself and others, and being willing to accept the results of your decisions, both the good and the not-so-good.

Here's how this balance works: When your parents let you walk to a friend's house by yourself, that's more freedom. The accountability part is that you need to arrive when you said you would and follow safety rules. If you show you can handle this responsibility, you might earn even more freedom later, like going to more places on your own.

Another example is managing your own homework. The freedom is that your parents don't remind you constantly or check every assignment. The accountability is that you're responsible for completing it on time and dealing with the consequences if you don't.

Finding this balance can be tricky sometimes. You might feel like you want all the freedom right away, but aren't quite ready for all the accountability that comes with it. Or adults in your life might not recognize when you're ready for more freedom.

The good news is that this balance shifts gradually. Each small responsibility you handle well builds trust, which often leads to more freedom. And each time you make a mistake but learn from it, you're showing that you can be accountable even when things don't go perfectly.

Common Fears and Misconceptions About Growing Up

Almost everyone has worries about growing up, even if they don't talk about them out loud. Let's look at some common fears and misconceptions many kids have—and the truth behind them:

Fear: "When I grow up, I'll have to give up fun and only do serious things."

- **Truth:** Adults definitely have responsibilities, but they also have fun! In fact, adults often have more freedom to enjoy their interests. They can stay up late watching movies, buy art supplies or video games with their own money, or spend a whole weekend doing their favorite hobby. Growing up means balancing responsibilities with things you enjoy—not giving up fun altogether.

Fear: "I need to know exactly what I want to be when I grow up."

- **Truth:** Very few people know their exact life path when they're young. Adults change careers many times throughout their lives! Right now, exploring different interests and developing skills you enjoy is more important than having your whole future figured out. Your dreams and goals will develop and change as you grow.

Fear: "Growing up means I'll stop being close to my family."

- **Truth:** Your relationship with your family will change as you grow up, but that doesn't mean you'll grow apart. Many people become closer to their parents when they get older, especially once they become adults themselves. The relationship evolves from parent-child to something more like a friendship while maintaining that special family bond.

Fear: "I'll have to figure everything out on my own."

- **Truth:** Even adults need help sometimes! Everyone continues to learn and rely on others throughout their lives. Teachers, parents, mentors, and friends will still be there to support you as you grow. Asking for help isn't a sign that you're not growing up; it's a mature thing to do.

Fear: "Growing up happens all at once, and I won't be ready."

- **Truth:** Growing up happens gradually, giving you time to adjust to each new stage. You don't go to bed as a child and wake up the next morning as a teenager with all new responsibilities. Each small step prepares you for the next one. By the time you reach a new stage, you'll have developed the skills you need.

Fear: "Everyone else seems ready to grow up except me."

- **Truth:** Almost everyone feels uncertain about growing up at times, even if they don't show it! Those classmates who seem so confident? They have worries too. Growing up is a journey with uncertain moments for everyone—you're definitely not alone in having mixed feelings about it.

Setting Goals for Yourself

We set goals so that we have a bit more direction; goals give us something to work towards, something to look forward to. Without them, you might wander around and have some fun adventures, but you might also miss out on reaching places that would make you really happy.

Setting goals doesn't mean planning every detail of your future right now. It just means thinking about what matters to you and taking steps in that direction.

Short-Term vs. Long-Term Goals

Goals come in different sizes:

Short-Term Goals
These are things you want to accomplish soon—in the next few days, weeks, or months. For example:

- learning to play a specific song on an instrument

- finishing a book series you're enjoying

- improving your soccer skills before the next season

- saving money for a special toy or game

Long-Term Goals

These are bigger dreams that might take years to achieve, like:

- learning to speak another language fluently

- becoming skilled enough at art to create detailed portraits

- getting into a particular middle or high school program

- visiting a certain country someday

Both types of goals are important! Short-term goals give you quick wins that keep you motivated, while long-term goals help you grow in meaningful ways over time.

Identifying Your Interests and Strengths

The best goals connect to things you either already enjoy or want to learn more about. Think about this:

- What activities make you lose track of time because you're having so much fun?

- What subjects or topics make you curious and eager to learn more?

- What do friends or family say you're particularly good at?

- What makes you feel proud when you accomplish it?

Your answers provide clues about the areas where setting goals might be especially rewarding for you.

Breaking Big Dreams Into Smaller Steps

A big goal like "becoming an author" might feel overwhelming. But breaking it into smaller steps makes it manageable:

1. Read lots of books in styles you enjoy.

2. Practice writing stories for 15 minutes three times a week.

3. Learn about one writing technique each month.

4. Share your stories with a trusted person for feedback.

5. Enter a writing contest or submit to a kids' magazine.

Each small step moves you toward your bigger dream while being achievable on its own.

Trying New Things to Discover Passions

Sometimes, you don't know what you'll love until you try it! Setting goals to explore new activities helps you discover interests you might never have expected:

- Try one new after-school activity each semester.

- Read books from genres you don't usually choose.

- Learn the basics of a skill that looks interesting but unfamiliar.

- Volunteer to help with different types of community projects.

The more experiences you have, the more you learn about what truly excites you.

Learning From Setbacks and Mistakes

Not every goal will go exactly as planned—and that's okay! When setbacks happen:

- Ask yourself what you can learn from the experience.

- Consider if your goal needs adjusting to be more realistic.

- Think about what support or resources might help you succeed next time.

- Remember that mistakes are part of everyone's journey toward their goals.

Many of the most successful people in the world faced numerous setbacks before achieving their dreams. Persistence often matters more than perfect performance!

Setting goals is a skill that gets better with practice. Start with a few small, achievable goals, celebrate when you reach them, and gradually challenge yourself with bigger dreams as you grow in confidence.

Practical Tools for Goal Achievement

Goals work better when they're noted or written down in places where we can see them. When your goals are just ideas floating around in your head, it's easy to forget about them or lose focus. But when you can actually see your goals every day, they stay fresh in your mind and keep you motivated to work toward them!

Vision Boards and Visual Reminders

A vision board is a fun way to make your goals visible. Here's how to create one:

1. Find a poster board, cork board, or even just a piece of paper.

2. Cut out pictures from magazines that represent your goals.

3. Add photos, drawings, quotes, or words that inspire you.

4. Hang your vision board somewhere you'll see it every day, like your bedroom wall.

You can make different types of visual reminders, too:

- a simple list of goals, decorated and posted above your desk

- a drawing that represents something you're working toward

- a calendar with milestone dates marked for tracking progress

- a jar where you add a marble or paper star each time you work on your goal

Looking at these visual reminders regularly helps keep your goals at the front of your mind.

Finding Mentors and Role Models

Having someone to guide you or inspire you makes reaching your goals much easier:

- Look for people you know who are good at what you want to learn.

- Ask a parent, teacher, or another trusted adult to help you find a mentor.

- Read biographies about people who have achieved similar goals.

- Watch interviews or documentaries about people you admire.

A mentor can

- give you specific advice based on their experience.

- help you avoid common mistakes.

- encourage you when things get tough.

- celebrate your successes with you.

Even if you can't find a personal mentor right away, learning from role models through books or videos can still provide valuable guidance and inspiration as you work toward your goals.

Remember that the tools that work best for you might be different from what works for your friends. Try a few different approaches and stick with the ones that keep you most motivated and excited about your goals!

Embracing Who You Are

You are you, and there's no one else like you. No one who laughs like you, no one who carries themselves in the way that you do, no one who has your exact combination of talents, interests, and perspectives. In all of human history, there has never been—and will never be—another person exactly like you.

Building a Positive Self-Image During Times of Change

When your body, emotions, and life circumstances are changing quickly, it can be challenging to maintain a positive view of yourself. One day you might feel confident and happy, and the next day uncomfortable in your own skin. This is completely normal during the growing-up years!

Building a positive self-image doesn't mean feeling perfect about yourself all the time. Instead, it means developing a realistic appreciation for who you are, including both your strengths and the areas where you're still growing.

Here are ways to nurture a positive self-image even during times of change:

- **Focus on what stays the same:** While many things about you are changing, your core qualities often remain consistent. Maybe you've always been kind, creative, determined, or good at making people laugh. Recognizing these continuing strengths gives you a sense of stability.

- **Celebrate your growth:** Notice and appreciate how you're developing and maturing. Focus on the little things, like the fact that you're becoming more responsible, braver about trying new things, or better at expressing your thoughts. These changes are achievements worth celebrating!

- **Practice self-compassion:** Don't be too harsh on yourself; there's already so much of that in the world around us. Instead of harsh self-criticism ("I look weird" or "I'm so stupid"), try gentle understanding ("My body is changing, and that's normal" or "Everyone makes mistakes sometimes").

- **Create a "strengths inventory":** Knowing what you're good at and what you excel in is so empowering. Kind of makes you feel like a super human. Make a list of things you're good at, personal qualities you're proud of, and positive feedback others have given you. Review this list when you're feeling unsure about yourself.

- **Look beyond appearance:** While it's natural to think about how you look as your body changes, remember that your appearance is just one small part of who you are. Your character, how you treat others, your interests and abilities—these aspects of yourself are even more important than how you look.

- **Find your "thing":** How wonderful is it that one day you're going to try something new and realize how happy this thing makes you. How much joy it conjures up in your heart. How lovely it is that you are still a person trying to find yourself. Having activities you enjoy and feel good at provides a strong foundation for your self-image. Whether it's a sport, art form, academic subject, or hobby, developing skills in areas you care about builds confidence that extends to other parts of your life.

- **Surround yourself with positive influences:** Spend time with people who appreciate you for who you are and who help you see your own strengths. Notice how you feel around different friends and family members, and try to spend more time with those who lift you up.

Remember that embracing who you are isn't about being perfect; it's about recognizing your unique value just as you are, while also growing into the person you want to become. Your journey of self-discovery will continue throughout your entire life, with each stage bringing new insights and appreciation for the amazing person you are.

Appreciate Your Body for What It Can Do, Not Just How It Looks

The next time you stand in front of a mirror, I want you to look at yourself and whisper these words: "Thank you, body. Thank you for carrying me through this day. Thank you for letting me run and jump and dance. Thank you for healing my scrapes and growing stronger with every challenge."

Our bodies are amazing, not because of how they look, but because of all the incredible things they do for us every single day. Your body is constantly working hard—pumping blood, breathing air, fighting off germs, and healing itself—all without you even having to think about it!

When you focus on what your body can *do* instead of just how it *looks*, you develop a deeper appreciation for it. Here are some amazing things your body does for you:

- Your brain processes more information than the world's most powerful computers.

- Your heart beats about 100,000 times every day without taking a break.

- Your lungs take in enough air to fill about 1,000 balloons each day.

- Your immune system fights off thousands of germs to keep you healthy.

- Your muscles allow you to move in countless ways, from delicate finger movements to powerful jumps.

- Your senses let you experience the beauty of music, the taste of your favorite foods, and the warmth of a hug.

When your body is changing in ways that you might not entirely understand, it is definitely going to feel uncomfortable, but don't forget to look and marvel at all the ways your body serves you.

Try this: Make a list of all the things you can do with your body that you couldn't do when you were younger. Maybe you can swim across the pool, reach the high shelves, carry your little sibling, or play a difficult piece of music. These abilities didn't come from how your body looks—they came from how it works and grows.

When you catch yourself focusing on appearance, gently redirect your thoughts to function and ability. Instead of *I don't like how my legs look*, try thinking, *My legs are strong enough to ride my bike up that big hill.* Instead of *My skin has pimples*, try *My skin protects all my internal organs and heals itself when I get a cut.*

This way of thinking helps you develop gratitude for your amazing body, no matter what shape, size, or stage of development it's in right now. Remember, your body's job isn't to look a certain way. Its job is to carry your wonderful spirit through the world and help you experience all life has to offer.

Continuing Lily's Story

On Saturday, Lily's family visited her aunt and uncle's house for cousin Tessa's birthday lunch. Lily had always admired Tessa, who seemed so confident in high school.

While adults prepared lunch, Lily found Tessa reading in a hammock in the backyard.

"Hey, squirt," Tessa said, making room. "Want to join me?"

After a comfortable silence, Lily asked, "Did you always know what you wanted to be when you grew up?"

Tessa laughed. "Are you kidding? I changed my mind like a hundred times."

"Really? But you always seem so sure about everything."

"When I was your age, I was totally confused," Tessa admitted. "Why? Are you worried about it?"

Lily explained her concerns about the writing assignment, middle school, and feeling like everyone else had life figured out.

"I don't even know what I'm good at anymore," Lily confessed. "Everything's changing too fast."

Tessa nodded. "It's like standing in a department store with too many choices and no idea what you need."

"Exactly! So what did you do?"

"I started making lists—not of careers, just things I was curious about. I called it my 'Maybe List'—things I might like to try or learn about."

"The cool thing is," Tessa continued, "when you write without judging, patterns appear. I realized many of my 'maybes' involved helping people or solving problems. That's how I got interested in engineering."

That night, Lily wrote "My Maybe List" in her journal:

Maybe I'd like to learn how to make videos.

Maybe I'd like to have a dog someday.

Maybe I'd like to visit Japan.

Over the next few days, her list grew to include potential careers, small curiosities, and dreams—without judging their practicality.

Reviewing her list later, Lily noticed many items involved creating things and helping people or animals.

She created a new page titled "Things I'm Excited About," focusing on near-future possibilities rather than career plans—having more freedom, learning to cook, going to movies with just friends.

Lily realized growing up didn't mean having all the answers immediately, but exploring possibilities and discovering what she loved along the way.

When sharing in class, Lily said, "I don't know exactly what I want to be yet, but I'm excited to try different things and figure it out. Right now, I'm just collecting possibilities."

That night, she added one more item:

Maybe growing up isn't as scary as I thought.

Your Time to Reflect

Letter to My Future Self

Write a letter to yourself five years from now. What would you like to tell your future self? What questions do you have?

Dear Future Me,

I'm writing to you from age _____, on date _____.

I'm curious about what your life is like now. Are you

_____?

Have you tried

_____?

Right now, I'm really good at

_____

I hope you still enjoy

_____

Something I'm working on improving is

_____

One thing I want you to remember about this time in your life is

_____

A question I have for you is

_____?

Take care of yourself!

Love,

_____

Journal Prompts

Use these questions to explore your thoughts about growing up:

- What three things are you most excited about for the future?

- What kind of person do you hope to become as you grow older?

- If you could learn any skill or talent, what would it be and why?

- Who is someone you admire, and what qualities do they have that you value?

- What makes you feel brave when facing new challenges?

My Future List

Just like Lily made her "Maybe List," create your own list of possibilities. These can be things you want to try, learn, visit, create, or become. Don't worry about whether they seem practical—just let your imagination flow!

Maybe I'd like to

_____

Maybe I'd enjoy

_____

Maybe I'd be good at

_____

Maybe I'd love to visit

_____

Maybe I'd want to learn

_____

Maybe I'd create

Lily's Letter to Her Future Self (Example)

Dear Future Lily,

I'm writing to you from age 11 on May 15th.

I'm curious about what your life is like now. Are you in high school? Do you have new friends? Is middle school as scary as everyone says?

Have you tried photography class yet? That's something I'm thinking about doing.

Right now, I'm really good at basketball and writing stories. I hope you still enjoy these things.

Something I'm working on improving is being more organized and speaking up when I have something to say.

One thing I want you to remember about this time in your life is that even though growing up feels confusing sometimes, you're figuring it out one day at a time. And that's okay!

A question I have for you is: Did you find something you're passionate about? Did any of the "maybes" on my list turn into something more?

Take care of yourself!

Love, Lily (your younger self)

My Growing Up Journey

Fill in milestones you've already reached and ones you're looking forward to:

Things I can do now that I couldn't do when I was younger:

_____

_____

Things I'm learning to do right now:

_____

_____

Things I look forward to being able to do:

_____

_____

My Special Qualities

Everyone has unique strengths and qualities that make them special. What are yours?

Three words that describe me:

1. _____

2. _____

3. _____

Something I do that helps others:

_____

Something that makes me unique:

_____

A challenge I've overcome:

_____

Remember that growing up is a journey, not a destination. There's no rush to figure everything out all at once!

CONCLUSION

D o you remember Lola and Rachel? Do you remember how they sat on those warm concrete steps, how they talked about the changes in their bodies and feelings? How Rachel was worried about getting a training bra, and Lola reassured her that everyone develops at their own pace?

Here's a plot twist: What if Lola, Rachel, and all the other girls you've met in this book—Mia, Lena, Emily, Jasmine, Sofia, Ava, and Lily—could all sit together in a circle, sharing their stories and little lessons? What do you think they would tell each other?

- Mia might talk about how she learned to handle body odor and found confidence in taking care of her changing body.

- Lena would share how scared she felt getting her first period at school, but how she now feels prepared with her period kit and knowledge.

- Emily would talk about how she went from feeling uncomfortable with her reflection to appreciating all the amazing things her body can do.

- Jasmine, maybe she would explain how she learned to hold her emotions and how she grew to accept their role in learning and maturing.

- Sofia would talk about navigating changing friendships and finding the courage to be herself even when facing social pressure.

- Ava would share how she's practicing standing up for herself and setting boundaries when something doesn't feel right.

- And Lily would tell everyone about her "Maybe List" and how she's discovering that growing up doesn't mean having all the answers right away.

Each girl's story is different, but they all share something important: they're learning, growing, and finding their way through the adventure of growing up.

You're on this journey, too! You may find that you relate to some of these girls' experiences more than others. You might be facing challenges that we haven't even addressed in this book. However, like these girls, you possess the ability to navigate this exciting, sometimes confusing, and always important time in your life.

Remember that your body is changing at the right pace for you. Your emotions, no matter how big and overwhelming they may feel, are a normal part of growing up. Your friendships might shift and evolve, but you'll learn which relationships truly matter. Most importantly, you're developing the strength, wisdom, and confidence to become your own wonderful and unique self.

The road ahead has twists and turns, ups and downs, but it's *your* road—and what an amazing journey it will be!

References

Ashley. (2021, August 19). *Why Girls' Social Struggles Intensify During Adolescence - Familius.com Shop.* Familius.com Shop. https://familius.com/why-girls-social-struggles-intensify-during-adolescence/?srsltid=AfmBOopjxoDR6i0AavbYHzxiu_ysnSTYSxGKJyQv8xjfFEb7zTKIjrj_

Bar soap vs. body wash. (2023). Jergens. https://mykaoshop.com/blogs/jergens/bar-soap-vs-body-wash?srsltid=AfmBOoqmaZsOubMvUoPUU1mRsc65LtoMYbrOBXHr9-EFh6pPEPJfWPTd

Breehl, L., & Caban, O. (2023). *Physiology, puberty.* Nih.gov; StatPearls Publishing. https://www.ncbi.nlm.nih.gov/books/NBK534827/

Clean and nearly teen: Personal hygiene. (n.d.). Stlouischildrens. https://www.stlouischildrens.org/health-resources/pulse/clean-and-nearly-teen-personal-hygiene

Eatough, E. (2022, April 5). *How to stand up for yourself: 8 ways to make it work.* Www.betterup.com. https://www.betterup.com/blog/how-to-stand-up-for-yourself

Five tips for healthy, glowing skin. (2022, January 22). Mayo Clinic. https://www.mayoclinic.org/healthy-lifestyle/adult-health/in-depth/skin-care/art-20048237

Friendship changes in the teenage years. (2021, September 16). Life Insight. https://life-insight.com/friendship-changes-in-the-teenage-years/

How to teach kids to love their bodies. (2021, January 7). DiveThru. https://divethru.com/how-to-teach-kids-to-love-their-bodies/

Hygiene for young people and teenagers. (2024). NHS. https://bedslutonchildrenshealth.nhs.uk/child-development-and-growing-up/hygiene/hygiene-for-young-people-and-teenagers/

Levine, I. (2025). *Handling a teenage daughter's friendship dramas.* Psychology Today. https://www.psychologytoday.com/us/blog/the-friendship-doctor/201010/handling-teenage-daughters-friendship-dramas

Mantle, A. (2023, March 14). *Personal hygiene checklist.* Health for Teens. https://www.healthforteens.co.uk/health/looking-after-your-body/personal-hygiene-checklist/

Marsh, P., Allen, J. P., Ho, M., Porter, M., & McFarland, F. C. (2006). The changing nature of adolescent friendships. *The Journal of Early Adolescence, 26*(4), 414–431. https://doi.org/10.1177/0272431606291942

McKay, L. (2023, May 18). *Twelve period products through history.* Natural Cycles. https://www.naturalcycles.com/cyclematters/period-products-through-history

Mitchell, D. (2022, May 16). *Tricky friendship days: Let's not dial down the drama.* Michelle Mitchell. https://michellemitchell.org/tricky-friendship-days-lets-not-dial-down-the-drama/?srsltid=AfmBOopcgSaUEDQ-Mfg-TrjGJoZnTP61eU7rmcRqwxFYEK9oTVBgE_by

Monroe, J. (2012, December 15). *The effects of teenage hormones on adolescent emotions.* Newport Academy; Newport Academy. https://www.newportacademy.com/resources/empo wering-teens/teenage-hormones-and-sexuality/

Physical changes in puberty: girls and boys. (2017, December 11). Raising Children Network. https://raisingchildren.net.au/pre-teens/development/puberty-sexual-development/physical-changes-in-puberty

Puberty: Tanner stages for boys and girls. (2023). Cleveland Clinic. https://my.clevelandclinic.org/health/body/puberty

Raypole, C. (2019, September 10). *List of emotions: 54 ways to say what you're feeling.* Healthline. https://www.healthline.com/health/list-of-emotions

Rebecca. (2025). *Letting go of the chase and reclaiming your self-worth.* Psychology Today. https://www.psychologytoday.com/za/blog/everyday -resilience/202503/letting-go-of-the-chase-and-reclaiming-your-self-worth

Rogers, S. (2024, October 29). *Understanding teenage mood swings: What's normal and when to get help.* Meridian HealthCare. https://meridianhealthcare.net/when-should-you-be-worried-about-teenage-mood-swings/

Stanborough, J. (2019, July 18). *How to use science-backed ways to get any smell out of your clothes.* Healthline. https://www.healthline.com/health/how-to-get-smell-out-of-clothes

Sutton, J. (2020, October 7). *Understanding emotions: 15 ways to discover what you're feeling.* Positive Psychology.

https://positivepsychology.com/understanding-emotions/

Teenage moods: the ups and downs of adolescence. (2022, October 20). Raising Children Network. https://raisingchildren.net.au/pre-teens/mental-health-physical-health/about-mental-health/ups-downs

Ten ways to teach preteen hygiene. (n.d.). Scholastic. https://www.scholastic.com/parents/family-life/kids-health/10-ways-to-teach-preteen-hygiene.html

Watson, K. (2020, September 28). *Bar soap vs. body wash: Which is better for the health of your skin?* Healthline. https://www.healthline.com/health/beauty-skin-care/bar-soap-vs-body-wash

White, K. (2018). *All about periods (for teens).* Kidshealth.org. https://kidshealth.org/en/teens/menstruation.html

Zaman, H. J. (2020, July 3). *Standing up for yourself is A skill- not A given.* Psych Central. https://psychcentral.com/blog/love-yourself/2020/07/standing-up-for-yourself-is-a-skill-not-a-given#1

Made in United States
Cleveland, OH
25 June 2025

17997624R00105